Canada College Library

W9-CUC-688

Writing in English: Step by Step

Written by Elizabeth Weal

Illustrated by Anastasia Ionkin

Tenaya Press

Palo Alto, CA

To the dedicated and hardworking students at Sequoia Adult School

©July, 2013 Elizabeth Weal

All inquiries should be addressed to
Elizabeth Weal
Tenaya Press
3481 Janice Way
Palo Alto, CA 94303

650-494-3941
ElizabethWeal@tenaya.com

Book design: Stuart Silberman
Cover: Beth Zonderman/Bruce Hodge
Cover photo: Mary Bender

About the cover

The quilt on the cover, which is from the collection of Mary Bender, was chosen because of its similarities to writing in English. While at first blush, the quilt appears somewhat haphazard, it in fact has a clear pattern with easily discernible interrelationships among its parts. My hope is that students whose writing once resembled a random ordering of words will, upon completing this book, understand that writing in English, like this quilt, possesses a discernible order and structure.

IBSN 978-0-9796128-2-4

Contents

To students

Writing in English is difficult. If English is your second language, it's even more difficult. This book tries to make writing as easy, painless, and fun as possible. I hope you enjoy it!

To teachers

I wrote this book for students whose written work looks like this:

> It was a busy day at the store. She was a talk on the phone. She not want buy candy for child. He wasn't early his date, he buy eggs but his child she play. One cashier is confuse he need a break. The store full and just it have open two lines.

I think of students like this as trying to make coq au vin without knowing how to boil an egg.

I wrote *Writing in English: Step by Step* to teach students to write clear, coherent, grammatically correct paragraphs—a skill that is a prerequisite for writing the longer, more in-depth, and more creative pieces that will be required of them when they take more advanced ESL and English classes.

The audience for this book is ESL students at the low intermediate level as well as native English speakers who, for whatever reason, didn't master rudimentary writing skills. It assumes students have been exposed to basic English grammar, including knowledge of subject pronouns, possessive adjectives, preposition of time and place, and simple present and present continuous verbs.

This book's methodology is simple; each chapter includes short lessons in grammar, sentence structure, and mechanics that students work through in preparation for an end-of chapter writing assignment that, in most cases, is based on a personal experience. Ending each chapter with a writing assignment is a key component of this book. I know from direct experience that learning a foreign language is a seemingly endless process. By completing a writing assignment using newly-acquired knowledge, students are reminded that they are indeed progressing.

As teachers know only too well, students, particularly those who have limited experience writing in their native language, rarely grasp grammar points the first time around. I address this issue by reviewing basic grammar during the early chapters of the book, while also focusing on mechanics, sentence structure, and content development. The final chapters introduce what for many students are new grammar constructs including past tense verbs, future tense verbs, verbs followed by prepositions, adverbs, conjunctions, and comparative adjectives.

Writing is a solitary activity. Yet students, regardless of what they're learning, thrive on interaction and engagement. Thus, while this book includes extensive writing exercises, it also provides a multitude of conversation activities. In some of these activities, students analyze text, comparing, for example, why one paragraph is clearer or more interesting than another. In other exercises, students engage in conversations in which they practice the same skills they're learning to apply to their written work.

How this book is organized

Each chapter in this book includes the following components:

- **Chapter opening:** As a class, students read and answer questions about a paragraph similar to the paragraph they will write as their end-of-chapter assignment.

- **Chapter content:** Each chapter includes several short lessons focusing on skills relating to mechanics, grammar, and sentence structure that students must use when they complete the end-of-chapter assignment.

- **Editing challenge**: Students edit a paragraph using the writing and editing skills they've learned in the current and previous chapters.

- **Preparing to write:** Students complete a pre-writing activity that facilitates their writing of the end-of-chapter assignment.

- **Writing assignment:** Students write a grammatically correct paragraph on an assigned topic. I strongly encourage you to require students to save each of their writing assignments or to save students' assignments for them. That way, after completing the book, students can look back on their work and take pride in what they've accomplished.

- **Editing check list:** Students verify the correctness of their paragraph before turning it in.

In writing this book, I tried to keep explanatory text to a minimum and focus on activities in which students learn by doing. These activities include:

- **Talk about it:** Working with a partner, students converse using the grammar and/or sentence structures being taught.

- **Think about it:** Working with a partner, students respond to short answer questions.

- **Write about it:** Working with a partner, students provide written answers to questions.

- **Practice:** Students work independently on written exercises.

Extending this book

To maximize the efficacy of this book you may want to incorporate the following additional activities.

Editing check-up: Start every class with an editing exercise. On the board, write sentences containing errors that are taken directly from students' writing assignments. Ask students to correct the errors and explain their corrections.

Peer editing: In addition to editing their own work, students edit the writing of their peers.

Partner swaps: Have students work with multiple partners for the *Talk about it* exercises. This cements the grammar point or sentence structure being introduced and also encourages students to interact with a variety of classmates.

Reader's theatre: After they have completed an assignment, students read their paragraphs aloud to their peers. Then students question each other about the paragraph's content. Another approach is to hold a Writer's Theatre once every few weeks in which students read their favorite assignments to the class.

Acknowledgements

The first five chapters of this book were developed as a result of a grant awarded to Sequoia District Adult School by the Silicon Valley Community Foundation to develop a writing curriculum that would better prepare adult school students for community college classes. Without that grant, this book may never have become a reality. Several colleagues at Sequoia District Adult School gave me valuable feedback on these initial chapters. Thank to Jim Brock, Barb Hooper, Maria Kleczewska, Barbara Lincoln, Marian Miller, and Judy Romines for your help and support.

I also want to thank Suzanne Huseman, Lorraine Ruston, and Wendy Vasquez who read through large portions of this book. Sandy Peterson read the complete manuscript and made many thoughtful comments which I incorporated. Julie Reis did a superb copy-editing job. Mary Bender and Bruce Hodge collaborated on the cover. Special thanks go to students in my summer, 2012 Level 3 ESL class--all of whom worked through the exercises and provided invaluable feedback.

Pre-tests, post-tests, and input

Please contact me at ElizabethWeal@tenaya.com if you would like a copy of a pre- and post-test to gauge what students have learned as a result of working through this book. I also want to encourage you to email me with comments and suggestions. One of the joys of being both author and publisher is that I can easily modify content to reflect input from you and your students, so don't hold back!

Chapter 1

All About Me

In this chapter you'll write about yourself.

Raymundo Chavez
January 14, 2013
Assignment 1

My name is Raymundo Chavez. I live in Detroit with my wife, my daughter, and two dogs. In my country I was a supervisor. Now, I am a construction worker. I live in a small apartment with a living room, bedroom, and a very small kitchen. One day I want to build my own house. I like the United States, but I don't like the snow and cold weather.

Answer each question with a complete sentence.

1. Where does Raymundo live? _____

_____

2. What is Raymundo's job? _____

_____

3. What is Raymundo's dream? _____

_____

4. Does Raymundo like the cold weather?_____

_____

Letters and words

The English alphabet has *26 letters*.

Letters	
capital letters	A B C D E F G H I J K L M N O P Q R S T U V W X Y Z
small letters	a b c d e f g h i j k l m n o p q r s t u v w x y z

You use letters to make *words*.

Words
boy   sleep   house   tire   Maria   book   beautiful   communication

Sentences

You use *words* to make *sentences*. All sentences start with a capital letter. A *statement* is a sentence that ends in a period. For example,

My sister is at home now.

A *question* is a sentence that ends with a question mark. For example,

What is your address?

Think about it

Work with a partner. Take turns. Read the following sentences out loud. Then answer the questions on the next page.

Sentences
1. I am tired.
2. The museum opens at 10 a.m.
3. Are you tired today?
4. Celia has two jobs.
5. How many students are there in your class?
6. I need to wash my clothes, dry my clothes, and sweep the floor.
7. You need to work tomorrow because Angela is on vacation.
8. Does your boss speak English?

1. Which is the longest sentence? How many words does it have? _____

_____

2. Which is the shortest sentence? How many words does it have? _____

_____

3. Which sentences are questions? _____ How do you know? _____

_____

Paragraphs

You use sentences to make *paragraphs*. A *paragraph* is a group of sentences about the same idea or *topic*.

Think about it

Work with a partner. Read the paragraph and answer the questions.

> Ana Cerda is 31 years old. She is from Oaxaca, Mexico. She is married. Her husband's name is Sam. Ana has two children. Enrique is 6, and Andrew is 4. She lives in Denver, Colorado.

1. What is the topic of this paragraph? _____
2. How many sentences are in this paragraph?_____

Paragraphs and lists

A paragraph is <u>not</u> a list. This is a list.

> My name is Victoria Alvarez.
>
> I'm from Miami, Florida.
>
> I'm 24 years old.
>
> I'm a babysitter.
>
> I want to be a teacher.

This is a paragraph.

> My name is Victoria Alvarez. I'm from Miami, Florida. I'm 24 years old. I'm a babysitter. I want to be a teacher.

Practice 1.1: This is a list. Write it as a paragraph.

     1. My name is James Phan.

     2. I am from Vietnam.

     3. I am 21 years old.

     4. I live with two roommates.

     5. I'm a construction worker.

     6. I want to get my GED.

       `My name is James Phan.`

_____

_____

_____

_____

_____

Think about it

Work with a partner. Identify each item in the table below. Write *word, sentence* or *paragraph*.

		What is this?
1.	mother	word
2.	The sky is blue.	
3.	You use grapes to make wine. Green grapes make white wine and purple grapes make red wine. Many different kinds of grapes grow in California.	
4.	Who is the president of your country?	
5.	The San Francisco Zoo is a very nice place to visit. There are many animals there including monkeys, elephants, lions, and tigers. The zoo is open seven days a week. Children under two are free.	
6.	Hawaii	
7.	At the grocery store, I need to buy milk, cheese, chicken, potatoes, eggs, bread, juice, cereal, and ice cream.	
8.	Life in the United States is good, but it is difficult. I have two jobs. I go to school. I am very busy.	
9.	What is your favorite color?	
10.	All students need to arrive at school on time. If you can't attend, call the office. If you're late, enter class quietly.	

More about paragraphs

Read this paragraph.

> The Golden Gate Bridge is very famous. It connects San Francisco and Marin County. The bridge opened in 1937. The bridge is orange so that ships can see it. About 100,000 vehicles cross the bridge every day.

Notice the following:

- All of the sentences are about the same topic, the Golden Gate Bridge.
- The second sentence continues on the first line. It does not start on a new line.
- There are five sentences in this paragraph.

Think about it

Work with a partner. Cross out the sentence that is not about the same topic as the other sentences. The first one is done for you.

Paragraph 1

> My sister is a pediatrician. She takes care of children. She works in a large clinic. ~~My brother lives in Mexico City.~~ My sister works hard. She works long hours. She sometimes works seven days a week. Fortunately, she also earns a lot of money.

Paragraph 2

> Los Angeles is very warm. The average temperature is 66 degrees during the day and 57 degrees at night. Los Angeles also is very dry. It only rains about 35 days each year. I like to swim. In Los Angeles the coldest month of the year is January. Of course, it never snows in Los Angeles.

Paragraph 3

> I like to go to the Lincoln Park Zoo with my husband and my daughter. I like to see the lions, tigers, and giraffes. My daughter likes the monkeys best. My daughter likes to play soccer. My husband likes the elephants best. I want to go to the zoo next month to see the animals.

Paragraph 4

Many teachers in the United States give homework every night. Some parents think homework is a good idea. They think that students need to study at home. Other parents don't like homework. They say that children should study at school and relax at home. My daughter is in fifth grade.

Paragraph 5

College campuses often are large. It is easy to get lost the first day of class. Before classes start, study a map of the campus. The first day of class, bring a campus map with you. I am nervous about college. If you get lost, ask another student for help.

Writing multiple paragraphs

There are two ways of showing paragraphs: *indented paragraphs* and *block paragraphs*. Look at the following examples.

Indented paragraphs

My Boyfriend, the Cook

My boyfriend Zach is a fantastic cook. He isn't a cook in a restaurant. He is a cook for his friends. He likes to cook breakfast, lunch, and dinner. When we have parties, Zach makes great food for everyone.

For breakfast, Zach makes delicious pancakes. His pancakes always have a special ingredient. He sometimes adds fruit like strawberries or peaches. He sometimes adds nuts or chocolate.

Zach loves salsa. But he never buys salsa. He always makes it. He always puts chiles in his salsa. It is very spicy.

I'm lucky to have a boyfriend who is a good cook. The problem is that I gained ten pounds.

Block paragraphs

My Boyfriend, the Cook

My boyfriend Zach is a fantastic cook. He isn't a cook in a restaurant. He is a cook for his friends. He likes to cook breakfast, lunch, and dinner. When we have parties, Zach makes great food for everyone.

For breakfast Zach makes delicious pancakes. His pancakes always have a special ingredient. He sometimes adds fruit like strawberries or peaches. He sometimes adds nuts or chocolate.

Zach loves salsa. But he never buys salsa. He always makes it. He always puts chiles in his salsa. It is very spicy.

I'm lucky to have a boyfriend who is a good cook. The problem is that I gained ten pounds.

Think about it

Work with a partner. Answer these questions about the story on the previous page.

1. Do indented paragraphs have a blank line after each paragraph? _____

2. Do block paragraphs have a blank line after each paragraph? _____

3. How many paragraphs are in the story *My Boyfriend, the Cook*? _____

4. How many sentences are in the first paragraph? _____

5. How many sentences are in the second paragraph? _____

6. How many sentences are in the third paragraph? _____

7. How many sentences are in the fourth paragraph? _____

8. What is the topic of the first paragraph? (Underline the best answer.)

    a. The author's boyfriend is a good cook

    b. The author likes to cook

    c. The author has a nice boyfriend

9. What is the topic of the second paragraph? (Underline the best answer.)

    a. Zach's pancakes

    b. Zach's favorite things to cook

    c. What Zach eats for breakfast

10. What is the topic of the third paragraph? (Underline the best answer.)

    a. Spicy food

    b. Zach's salsa

    c. chocolate pancakes

11. What is the topic of the fourth paragraph? (Underline the best answer.)

    a. The author likes to cook.

    b. The author is overweight

    c. The author is happy because her boyfriend is a good cook.

12. What is the topic of this story? (Underline the best answer.)

    a. How to gain weight

    b. Zach, a very good cook

    c. How to make good pancakes

13. Look at a newspaper or book. Does it use indented paragraphs or block paragraphs?

_____

_____

Practice 1.2: Read each paragraph. Then underline the information in the box that is included in each paragraph. The first item is underlined for you.

Paragraph 1

      I want to introduce myself. My name is Gerardo Gomez. I am from El Salvador. I am married. I have one daughter. Her name is Erika. I am a construction worker. I want to be a carpenter. I played soccer every Saturday in my country. Now I am too busy.

<u>name</u>	goal
marital status	where he lives
family	hobbies
native country	languages
current job	school/college
age	friends

Paragraph 2

      I want to introduce myself. My name is Raymundo Garcia. I am 21 years old. I'm a student at Omaha City College. I want to be a nurse. I am single. I live with two friends in an apartment in Omaha.

name	goal
marital status	where he lives
family	hobbies
native country	languages
current job	school/college
age	friends

Paragraph 3

      I want to introduce myself. My name is Anita Lopez. I live in Seattle with my daughter and my sister. I love to cook. In my country, I owned a restaurant. It was called Dos Tamales. One day I want to open a restaurant in the United States.

name	goal
marital status	where she lives
family	hobbies
native country	languages
current job	school/college
age	friends

Paragraph 4

      I want to introduce myself. My name is May Trong. I live in San Francisco. I am single. I live with my sister. My parents live in Los Angeles. I love to draw and I like the museums in San Francisco. I am a graphic designer.

name	goal
marital status	where she lives
family	hobbies
native country	languages
current job	school/college
age	friends

Talk about it

Ask your partner the following questions:

1. What is your name?

2. What is your marital status?

3. How old are you?

4. What are your hobbies?

5. Where do you live?

6. What languages do you speak?

Writing Assignment 1: Preparing to write

Write 6 or more sentences about yourself. Use the paragraphs on the previous page as examples.

1. My name is _____

2. I am from _____

3. I speak _____

4. _____

   _____

5. _____

   _____

6. _____

   _____

7. _____

   _____

8. _____

   _____

Using correct format

When you write a paragraph, you use a special *format*. Here is the format you will use.

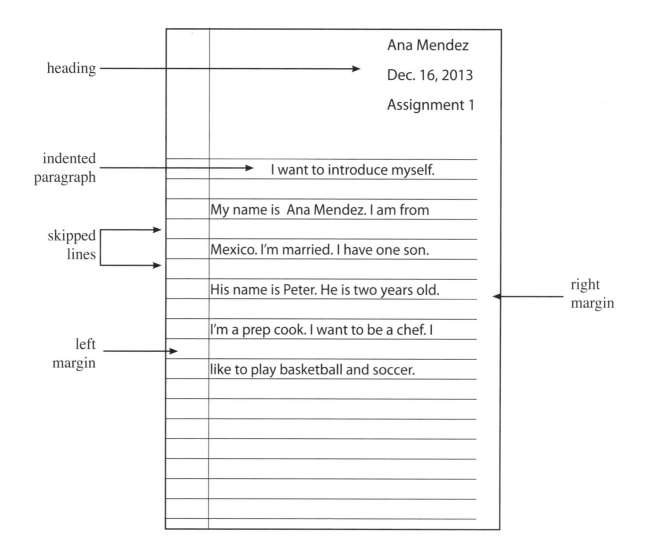

Notice the following:

- The heading goes in the upper right corner. It includes your name, the date, and the assignment number.

- There is a *left margin* and a *right margin*. Do not write in the margins.

- The first line of the first paragraph is *indented*. That means that you leave space before you start writing.

- The author *skipped lines*. That means there is a blank line after every line of writing.

Writing Assignment 1: *All About Me*

Write a paragraph about yourself. Use the format on the previous page. Follow these steps:

1. In the top right corner of your paper write:

    Your first and last name

    Today's date

    Assignment 1

2. Indent.

3. Begin the paragraph like this:

    I want to introduce myself.

4. Write your paragraph. Copy the sentences you wrote on page 9. Skip lines.

5. Start each sentence with a capital letter. End each sentence with a period.

6.. Use the editing checklist below to check your paragraph. Circle *Yes* or *No* for each item.

Writing Assignment 1: Editing Checklist

Editing Checklist		
Format		
1. My complete name, the date, and the assignment number are in the top right corner of the paper.	Yes	No
2. The first line is indented.	Yes	No
3. The sentences are in a paragraph. They are not in a list.	Yes	No
4. I skipped lines.	Yes	No
Content		
1. All of the sentences are about me.	Yes	No
2. My paragraph has at least 6 sentences.	Yes	No
Punctuation and capitalization		
1. I used capital letters correctly.	Yes	No
2. I ended each sentence with a period.	Yes	No

Chapter 2

All About My Classmate

In this chapter you'll write about a classmate.

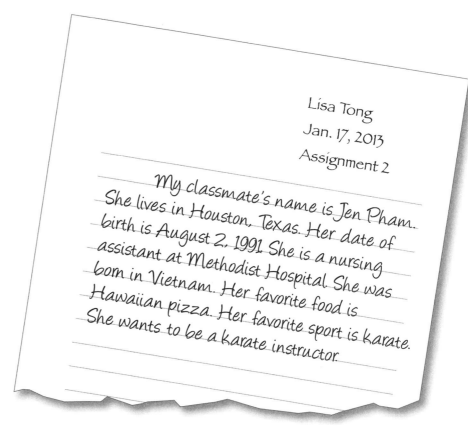

Lisa Tong
Jan. 17, 2013
Assignment 2

My classmate's name is Jen Pham. She lives in Houston, Texas. Her date of birth is August 2, 1991. She is a nursing assistant at Methodist Hospital. She was born in Vietnam. Her favorite food is Hawaiian pizza. Her favorite sport is karate. She wants to be a karate instructor.

Answer each question with a complete sentence.

1. Where is Jen from? _____

_____

2. How old is Jen? _____

_____

3. What is Jen's goal? _____

_____

4. What is Jen's favorite sport?_____

_____

Capital letters and small letters

English has two kinds of letters: *capital letters* and *small* or *lowercase letters*.

Letters	
capital letters	A B C D E F G H I J K L M N O P Q R S T U V W X Y Z
small letters	a b c d e f g h i j k l m n o p q r s t u v w x y z

Use a capital letter at the beginning of a word. The following are <u>not</u> correct:

- ~~hELlo~~
- ~~ChrisTMas~~
- ~~oRAngE~~

The only time you use capital letters in the middle or end of a word is in some abbreviations. Here are some examples:

Complete name	Abbreviation
the United States of America	the USA
identification card	ID card
television	TV

Practice 2.1: Cross out each word that includes incorrect capital letters. Then rewrite the word. Remember that the first word in a sentence starts with a capital letter.

```
cousin
```
My ~~couSin~~ is a coLLege stUdent. Her name is Amanda. She is TakiNG two claSSes.

Her First class is maTH. Her Second claSS is bioLogy. One day She wANts to be A nuRSe. She

liKeS college but It is diFFiculT. She also hAs a part time job. Right now, she doesn't have a

lot of free Time.

Capital letters at the beginning of a sentence

The first letter of the first word in a sentence is always a capital letter.

Think about it

Work with a partner. Correct this paragraph so that the first word in each sentence starts with a capital letter.

Florida is a beautiful state. it is called the Sunshine State because it is usually warm and sunny. every year, millions of people visit Orlando, Florida to go to Disney World. the largest city in Florida is Jacksonville. miami is also an important city in Florida. about sixty percent of the people in Miami are Latinos. most of these people came from Cuba.

When to use capital letters

This chart tells you when you use capital letters in English.

Use a capital letter for	Examples
The pronoun **I**	Susana and I are sisters.
Names of people	Alberto Cortez Mendoza
Titles of people	Mr. Wilson, Mrs. Johnson, Miss Mendez, Aunt Lucy
Days of the week	Tuesday
Months of the year	March
Cities, states, and countries	Houston, California, United States, Nicaragua, China
Street names	34 Green Street
Names of specific places	Target, Denny's, The San Francisco Zoo
Holidays	Christmas, Halloween
Languages	English, Spanish, Chinese
Nationalities	American, Mexican, Chinese
Brand names	Toyota, Pepsi, Sony
The first letter of the first word in a sentence	The ice cream is delicious.

You don't start the names of jobs with a capital letter. This sentence is correct.

I am a cook.

This sentence is not correct.

I am a ~~Cook.~~

Practice 2.2: Change the small letters to capitals when necessary.

1. Ning is from china.

2. Last year, i went to santiago, chile.

3. Her parents live on university avenue.

4. the students are from many countries including china, india, and mexico.

5. Olga lived in florida for five years.

6. I have a doctor's appointment on tuesday, may 26th.

7. My children and i like to go to pizza hut for dinner.

8. Next year, i want to go to my country for christmas.

9. On thursday he will meet his friend luis at starbucks.

10. My daughter attended west valley college for three years.

More about capital letters

You only use capital letters to talk about specific places. Read these sentences.
- I need to go to Chavez Market to buy food.
- I need to go to the market to buy food.

In the first sentence, *Chavez* and *Market* start with capital letters because *Chavez Market* is the name of a specific place. In the second sentence, *market* does not start with a capital letter because it is not the name of a specific place.

Now read these sentences.
- I live on Green Street.
- I live on a busy street.

In the first sentence, *Green* and *Street* start with capital letters because *Green Street* is the name of a specific street. In the second sentence, *street* does not start with a capital letter because it is not the name of a specific street.

Talk about it

Work with a partner. Read these sentences. Then answer the questions.

- Susan went to Bixby Park last weekend.
- Susan went to the park last weekend.

1. In the first sentence, ***Bixby Park*** is capitalized. Why?

2. In the second sentence, ***park*** isn't capitalized. Why?

Think about it

Work with a partner. Each sentence has one capitalization error. Find the error and correct it.

1. I like to go to the Park after work.

2. My sister works at costco.

3. I need to go to the Store to buy food.

4. I need to go to Chavez market to buy milk for dinner.

5. Can you take me to target after work?

6. The food at Taco bell is cheap.

7. Is your car a toyota?

8. My husband goes to School five nights a week.

9. My son studied spanish in Chile.

10. I need to go to walgreens to buy medicine.

11. Hoover School is located in Redwood City, california.

12. I'm going to hillsdale Mall to buy new shoes.

13. My mother and father live in cambodia.

14. Sequoia Adult School is located on Middlefield road.

15. It is very hot in the Summer.

Using commas

Use a comma between a city and a country.

> I am from San Paolo, Brazil.

Use a comma between a city and a state.

> I am from Springfield, Illinois.

Use a comma between the day and the year.

> I was born on June 3, 1989.

Do not use a comma at the end of a sentence. Use a period at the end of a sentence. This is correct.

> My classmate's name is Amanda Johnson. She is from Mexico.

This is *not* correct.

> My classmate's name is Amanda Johnson, She is from Mexico.

Practice 2.3: Each sentence has one comma error. Find the error and correct it.

1. My husband is from Lima Peru.

2. I have two sisters, Both sisters are in my country.

3. Andrew's date of birth is July 3 2001.

4. The party is on August, 5.

5. Your shoes are under the bed, Your coat is in the closet.

6. Her boss is from Miami Florida.

7. The cherries are cheap, The bananas are expensive.

8. I want to visit Managua Nicaragua.

9. Angelica was born on May 14 1996.

10. Paris France is a beautiful city.

Editing challenge

Now you're ready to practice what you've learned.

- Read the personal information form about Nisha Gupta.
- Correct the errors in the paragraph on the next page. There are 23.
- Rewrite the paragraph on the next page.
- Answer the questions on the next page.

Personal Information About <u>Nisha Gupta</u>

Street address: 44 Green Street

City: Athens   **State:** Georgia   **Zip:** 30603

School: Fairwood Adult School

Occupation: medical assistant

Place of employment: Fairmont Hospital

Date of birth: July 22, 1980

Place of birth: New Delhi, India

Favorite kind of food: Indian

Favorite restaurant: Delhi Kitchen

Favorite sport: volleyball

Goal: nurse

My classmate's name is Nisha Gupta. Her address is 44 ~~green~~ ^{Green} street, athens

georgia, 34321. her date of birth is july 22 1980. she was born in New Delhi, india.

she is a Medical Assistant. she works at fairmont hospital. her favorite kind of food is

indian. her favorite sport is volleyball. her favorite restaurant is pizza hut. One day She

wants to be a Nurse.

`My classmate's name is Nisha Gupta. Her`

_____

_____

_____

_____

_____

_____

_____

Answer with a complete sentence.

1. Where does Nisha work? _____

_____

2. What is Nisha's favorite kind of food? _____

_____

3. What is Nisha's goal? _____

_____

4. How many sentences are there in this paragraph? _____

_____

Writing Assignment 2: Preparing to write

Interview a classmate and complete this personal information form. Remember to use capital letters correctly.

Personal Information about _____

Street address: _____

City: _____ State: _____ Zip: _____

School: _____

Occupation: _____

Place of employment: _____

Date of birth: _____ Place of birth (city, country): _____

Favorite kind of food: _____

Favorite restaurant: _____

Favorite sport: _____

Goal: _____

Write about it

Write between 7 and 10 sentences about your classmate. Use the information from the chart above.

1. _____

2. _____

3. _____

4. _____

5. _____

6. _____

7. _____

8. _____

9. _____

10. _____

Writing Assignment 2: *All About My Classmate*

1. In the top right corner of your paper write:

> Your first and last name
>
> Today's date
>
> **Assignment 2**

2. Indent.

3. Begin the paragraph like this:

> My classmate's name is _____

4. Write your paragraph. Use the sentences you wrote on the previous page. Skip lines.

5. Start each sentence with a capital letter. End each sentence with a period.

6. Use the editing checklist. Circle *Yes* or *No* for each item.

Writing Assignment 2: Editing Checklist

Editing Checklist		
Format		
1. My complete name, the date, and the assignment number are in the top right corner of the paper.	Yes	No
2. The first line is indented.	Yes	No
3. Sentences are in a paragraph. They are not in a list.	Yes	No
4. I skipped lines.	Yes	No
Content		
1. My paragraph has between 7 and 10 sentences.	Yes	No
2. All of the sentences are about my classmate.	Yes	No
Capitalization and punctuation		
1. I used capital letters correctly.	Yes	No
2. I ended each sentence with a period.	Yes	No
3. I used commas correctly.	Yes	No

Chapter 3

A Typical Day

In this chapter you'll write about a classmate's typical day.

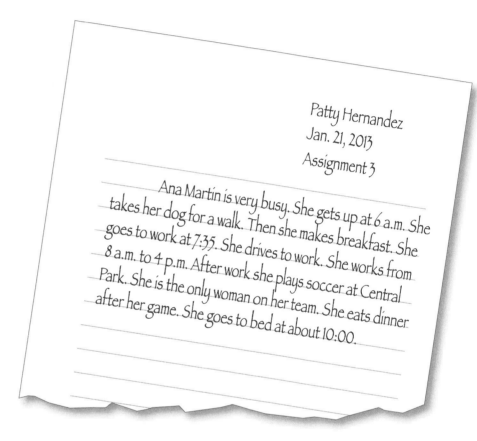

Patty Hernandez
Jan. 21, 2013
Assignment 3

Ana Martin is very busy. She gets up at 6 a.m. She takes her dog for a walk. Then she makes breakfast. She goes to work at 7:35. She drives to work. She works from 8 a.m. to 4 p.m. After work she plays soccer at Central Park. She is the only woman on her team. She eats dinner after her game. She goes to bed at about 10:00.

Answer each question with a complete sentence.

1. What time does Ana go to work? _____

_____

2. What kind of pet does Ana have? _____

_____

3. Is Ana the only woman on her soccer team? _____

_____

4. Where does Ana play soccer? _____

_____

Identifying verbs

To write correct sentences and paragraphs in English you need to know how to identify nouns, pronouns, adjectives, and verbs. First, we'll talk about verbs. There are two kinds of verbs:

- Verbs that show action (for example, *walk*, *talk*, *sing*)

- Verbs that do not show action (for example, *like*, *want*, *feel*, *need*, *be*)

Talk about it

Work with a partner. Make a list of 14 verbs.

1. cook	8.
2.	9.
3.	10.
4.	11.
5.	12.
6.	13.
7.	14.

Practice 3.1: Put two lines under the verb in each sentence. The first one is done for you.

1. I <u>live</u> in Japan.

2. My parents work in San Francisco.

3. The students write an essay once a week.

4. I sweep the floor in the morning and in the afternoon.

5. The bus leaves for Reno at 4:30.

6. I am in love.

7. We need apples, carrots, and beans.

8. The students want more homework.

9. I watch TV in the evening.

10. My boyfriend's birthday is June 23.

11. My daughter always buys her clothes at Target.

12. Sylvia feeds her dog twice a day.

Simple present tense verbs

Verbs can be in the past, present, or future. In this chapter, we talk about *simple present tense* verbs.

You use *simple present tense* verbs to

- talk about activities you do regularly (For example, **Luis** <u>works</u> *five days a week.*)

- talk about facts (For example, **I** <u>have</u> *two children.*)

There are two forms of simple present tense verbs: the *base form*, and the *"s"* form.

When to use the base form	When to use the "s" form
I eat	he eat<u>s</u>, Juan eat<u>s</u>
you eat	she eat<u>s</u>, Lucy eat<u>s</u>
we eat, Ana and I eat	it eat<u>s</u>, my fish eat<u>s</u>
they eat, the students eat, John and Jose eat	

Note the following:
- In the simple present tense, you add an *s* to the base verb after **he**, **she**, **it**, one person or one thing. You use the base form of the verb all other times.
- The simple present tense of *have* is irregular. The *"s"* form is **has.** It's not ~~haves.~~
- The simple present tense of *go* is irregular. The *"s"* form is **goes**. It's not ~~gos.~~
- The simple present tense of *do* is irregular. The *"s"* form is **does**. It's not ~~dos.~~
- The simple present tense of *to be* is irregular. The *"s"* form is **is**. It's not ~~bes.~~
- See Appendix A for rules about spelling simple present tense verbs.

Think about it

Read these sentences with a partner. Then circle the correct verb.

1. She (like, likes) Mexican food.

2. I (live, lives) in an apartment on 5th Avenue.

3. Those cell phones (need, needs) new batteries.

4. They (use, uses) the computer every day.

5. Nick (call, calls) his mother once a week.

6. The students (want, wants) more homework.

7. My sister and I (go, goes) to the mall every weekend.

8. Anthony (have, has) many friends in the United States.

9. The class (end, ends) at noon.

10. Mario (play, plays) the piano very well.

Practice 3.2: Look at Amanda's schedule. Then write four more sentences about Amanda's daily routine. Remember to put *at* before each time.

Amanda's schedule	
Time	**Activity**
6:30	get up
7:15	take a shower
7:45	make breakfast
8:00	eat breakfast
8:30	take her children to school
9:00	arrive at work

1. <u>Amanda gets up at 6:30.</u>

2. _____

3. _____

4. _____

5. _____

Identifying nouns

A *noun* is a person, animal, place, or thing. Read this sentence. The nouns are underlined.

- <u>Ana</u> went to the <u>store</u> to buy <u>food</u> for her <u>dog</u>.

Notice the following:

- Ana is a noun because it is a person.
- store is a noun because it is a place.
- food is a noun because it is a thing.
- dog is a noun because it is an animal.

Think about it

Work with a partner. Write 16 nouns.

1. <u>clock</u>	9. _____
2. _____	10. _____
3. _____	11. _____
4. _____	12. _____
5. _____	13. _____
6. _____	14. _____
7. _____	15. _____
8. _____	16. _____

Think about it

Work with a partner. Read each sentence. Then,

- Write each noun.
- Write if the noun is a person, place, animal, or thing.

	Noun	Is this noun a person, place, animal, or thing?
1. Ana has a headache.	Ana	person
	headache	thing
2. The students go to school in Seattle.		
3. My bedroom has two beds and one dresser.		
4. My dog likes ice cream.		
5. Quick Stop Market is on Grant Road.		
6. Andrea and Martin went to a Chinese restaurant in San Francisco.		
7. The cooks work at Hobee's Restaurant.		
8. My daughter wants a cat for her birthday.		
9. My classroom has large windows and many desks.		
10. New York has many tall buildings and interesting museums.		

Singular and plural nouns

A noun can be *singular* or *plural*. Most nouns form the plural by adding **s**.

singular noun	plural noun
book	books
cellphone	cellphones

Some nouns have *irregular plurals*. Here are some examples.

singular noun	irregular plural noun
woman	women
man	men
child	children
person	people

See Appendix A for spelling rules for plural nouns.

Using *A* and *An*

To refer to a singular noun or an adjective that starts with a consonant, use **a**. To refer to a singular noun or an adjective that starts with a vowel, use **an.**

I have <u>a</u> computer.   I have <u>a</u> new car.

I have <u>an</u> apple.   We have <u>an</u> interesting class.

Common mistakes with single and plural nouns

Don't forget the **s** on plural nouns.

Incorrect	Correct
Tran has two ~~sister.~~	Tran has two <u>sisters.</u>

Use **a** and **an** with singular nouns. Do not use **a** and **an** with plural nouns.

Incorrect	Correct
We are ~~a~~ students.	We are students.

Don't add **s** to irregular plural nouns.

Incorrect	Correct
We have two ~~childrens.~~	We have two <u>children.</u>

Think about it

- If the sentence is correct, put an X in the *Correct* box.

- If the sentence is incorrect,

  - Put an X in the *Incorrect* box.

  - Correct the sentence.

	Correct	Incorrect
1. We have apples and a ~~bananas.~~ banana		X
2. Ana has two a sisters.		
3. I need a key.		
4. We need light bulb.		
5. You can rent a cars at the airport.		
6. Lisa is a excellent student.		
7. My brother needs a job.		
8. There are a students in the classroom.		
9. My city has a new library.		
10. The childrens are late.		
11. You can buy organic egg at Midtown Market.		
12. My aunt is a beautiful women.		
13. I have a apricot in my backpack.		
14. My parents have three cat and one dog.		

Talk about it

Ask your partner the following questions. Respond with *I have....*

- What is in your pockets?

- What is in your backpack or purse?

- What is in your closet at home?

Subjects and verbs

A *sentence* is a group of words that expresses an idea. Every sentence has a *subject* and a *verb*. This is the form.

Subject	Simple present verb	Rest of the sentence
Angelica	lives	in Texas.

In the sentence above, the verb is ***lives***. The subject is ***Angela***.

The subject can be more than one word. Here is an example.

Subject	Simple present verb	Rest of the sentence
Luis and Jorge	work	at Pop's Pizza.

Talk about it

Tell your partner six sentences. Use a word from each column.

Subject	Verb	Rest of sentence
Cecilia	is/are	Mexican food
Ang	have/has	pizza
My sister	eat/eats	in Chicago
My friends	work/works	in Los Angeles
My friend	live/lives	at home
Erica and Louis	like/likes	two jobs
		alone

Write about it

Work with your partner. Write six sentences from the list above. Use words from each column.

1. <u>Cecilia is in Chicago.</u>

2. _____

3. _____

4. _____

5. _____

6. _____

Using nouns and pronouns

A *subject pronoun* is a word that replaces a noun that is the subject of a sentence. Read this sentence.

> Angela works five days a week.

The subject, **Angela**, is a noun. Now read this sentence.

> She works five days a week.

The subject, **she**, is a subject pronoun.

There are seven subject pronouns in English.

Singular	Plural
I	we
you	you
he	they
she	
it	

Use **you** to refer to one person or more than one person.

> You are a student.
> You are students.

Use **they** for both people and things.

> The students are tired. <u>They</u> work all day.
> The flowers are beautiful. <u>They</u> smell wonderful.

In the first example, **they** refers to **students**, a plural noun that refers to people. In the second example, **they** refers to **flowers**, a plural noun that refers to things.

Think about it

Work with a partner.

1. How many subject pronouns are there in English? _____

2. In English are there more nouns or subject pronouns? _____

3. Write N if the word is a noun. Write P if the word is a subject pronoun.

a. books	__N__	f. uncle	_____
b. potatoes	_____	g. we	_____
c. they	_____	h. rain	_____
d. I	_____	i. apartment	_____
e. Louisa	_____	j. newspaper	_____

Practice 3.3

- Put two lines under the verb in each sentence.
- Put one line under the subject of each sentence.
- Write **N** if the subject is a noun. Write **P** if the subject is a pronoun.

1. <u>Jessica</u> <u>has</u> two jobs. _(N)_

2. My sister plays soccer every week.

3. My family watches TV together every night.

4. Tigers are dangerous animals.

5. It costs $500.

6. Our class ends at 8:30.

7. My teacher needs more markers in her classroom.

8. The students are very noisy.

9. He usually works late on Tuesdays.

10. My sister and brother-in-law live in Colorado.

11. It is cold in Alaska.

12. In my country the children go to school six days a week.

13. My boss never listens to me.

14. The students clean the tables every day before class.

15. On Wednesdays we work late.

16. Phil, Lucy, Maria, Fred, and Heather are already at the party.

17. Angela goes to salsa parties every weekend.

18. On Mondays Max lifts weights at the gym.

19. The apples, oranges, and bread are still in the bag on the counter.

20. My niece swims in the pond near her house.

Missing subjects

Don't forget to include *it* and ***they*** when they are the subject of a sentence. You use *it* when the subject is singular and is a thing. For example

My car is old. <u>It</u> is broken.

Use ***they*** when the subject is plural and is a person or a thing. For example,

My parents are old. <u>They</u> are healthy.

My boots are old. <u>They</u> are very dirty.

Practice 3.4: Rewrite each sentence so it is a complete sentence. Add *It* or ***They***.

1. My garden is lovely. _____ has many flowers.

2. The flowers are beautiful. _____ are many different colors.

3. _____ is my birthday today.

4. These books are interesting. _____ are from the library.

5. My backpack is new. _____ is from Target.

6. My socks are new. _____ are from Ross.

7. _____ is cold today.

8. My pets are hungry. _____ need food.

9. My uncle built his own house. _____ looks beautiful.

10. My parents work very hard. _____ often work seven days a week.

11. The computers in the classroom are very old. _____ are often broken.

12. Today is my sister's birthday. _____ also is my anniversary.

13. Melissa, Ana, and Barbara are old friends. Now _____ live in different cities.

14. You need to take off your shoes at the door. _____ are very dirty.

15. The students are late. _____ missed the bus.

Complete and incomplete sentences

In English, every sentence has a *subject* and a *verb*. A sentence with a subject and verb is a *complete sentence*. A sentence without a subject and verb is an *incomplete sentence*.

Talk about it

The sentences below are **not** complete sentences. Tell your partner why.

> I two brothers.

> am from Mexico.

> Los Angeles a big city.

Think about it

- If the sentence is complete, put an X in the *Complete* box.
- If the sentence is incomplete,
  - Put an X in the *Incomplete* box.
  - Correct the sentence.
  - In the *Problem* box, write **no subject** or **no verb**.

	Complete	Incomplete	Problem
am 1. I tired today.		X	No verb
2. She has two jobs.	X		
3. My keys on the table.			
4. I two children.			
5. We live in San Francisco.			
6. Is late.			
7. They have three cats.			
8. I ready.			
9. Are sick.			
10. I have a son. Is very smart.			
11. They ready now.			
12. We late.			

Editing challenge

Now you're ready to practice what you've learned.

- Correct the errors in this paragraph. Each error is underlined.
- Rewrite the paragraph.
- Answer the questions below.

Caroline's day is very busy. She gets up <u>7:00</u>. She takes a shower. She <u>have</u> breakfast. She eats two <u>egg</u> and a piece of bacon. At 7:45 her children <u>gets up</u>. Caroline <u>make</u> breakfast for her children. <u>Drives</u> her children to <u>school, then</u> she comes home and <u>clean</u> her house. At 1:00 she <u>go</u> to work. She works at <u>taco loco</u>. <u>after</u> work she comes home and <u>help</u> <u>your</u> children with their <u>homework At</u> 10:00 <u>She go</u> to <u>Bed</u>. <u>She very</u> tired.

<pre>
                Caroline's day is very busy.
</pre>

_____

_____

_____

_____

_____

_____

_____

_____

Answer with a complete sentence.

1. What time does Caroline go to work? _____

_____

2. Where does Caroline work? _____

_____

3. Does Caroline have children? _____

_____

Writing Assignment 3: Preparing to write

Fill in the form below. Ask your classmate about a typical day. For example,

What time do you eat breakfast?

Include at least 10 activities. Use these verbs to help you.

get up	eat	wash (dishes, clothes)	drive	clean
get dressed	drink (coffee, milk)	go (home, to work, to school)	watch (TV)	call
brush (your hair, your teeth)	prepare (breakfast, lunch, dinner)	arrive (home, at work, at school)	relax	talk to
listen (to music)	work	leave (home, work, school)	help	go (to sleep)
take (a shower)	study	pick up	exercise	do (homework, dishes)

_____ schedule	
(name)	
time	**activity**
	`gets up`
	`takes a shower`

Write about it

Write between 7 and 10 sentences about your classmate's typical day. Use the information from the chart on the previous page.

1. _____

2. _____

3. _____

4. _____

5. _____

6. _____

7. _____

8. _____

9. _____

10. _____

Writing Assignment 3: *A Typical Day*

Write a paragraph about your classmate's typical day. Follow these steps:

1. In the top right corner of your paper write:

   Your first and last name

   Today's date

   Assignment 3

2. Indent.

3. Begin the paragraph:

   _____ day is very _____ (*quiet*, *busy*, *active*, *boring*)

4. Write your paragraph. Use sentences from the list above. Write between 7 and 10 sentences.

5. Skip lines.

6. Start each sentence with a capital letter. End each sentence with a period.

7. Use the editing checklist to check your paragraph. Circle **Yes** or **No** for each item.

Writing Assignment 3: Editing Checklist

Editing Checklist		
Format		
1. My complete name, the date, and the assignment number are in the top right corner of the paper.	Yes	No
2. I indented.	Yes	No
3. The sentences are in a paragraph. They are not in a list.	Yes	No
4. I skipped lines.	Yes	No
Content		
1. All of the sentences are about a typical day.	Yes	No
2. The paragraph has between 7 and 10 sentences.	Yes	No
Punctuation and capitalization		
1. I used capital letters correctly.	Yes	No
2. I ended each sentence with a period.	Yes	No
Grammar		
1. Simple present tense verbs that refer to *he*, *she*, or *it* or one person or thing end in an *s*.	Yes	No
2. Each sentence has a subject and a verb.	Yes	No

Chapter 4

My Weekend

In this chapter you'll write about your weekend.

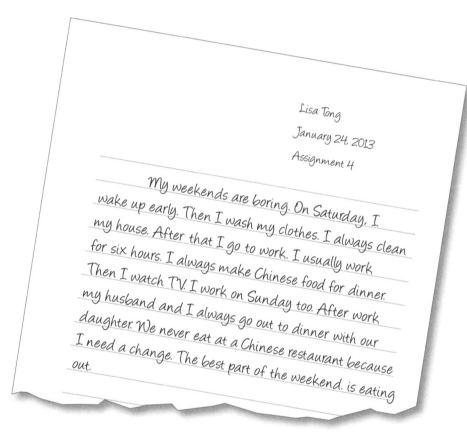

Lisa Tong

January 24, 2013

Assignment 4

My weekends are boring. On Saturday, I wake up early. Then I wash my clothes. I always clean my house. After that I go to work. I usually work for six hours. I always make Chinese food for dinner. Then I watch TV. I work on Sunday too. After work my husband and I always go out to dinner with our daughter. We never eat at a Chinese restaurant because I need a change. The best part of the weekend. is eating out.

Answer each question with a complete sentence.

1. Does Lisa have exciting weekends? _____

2. What does Lisa do on Saturday after she cleans her house? _____

_____

3. When does Lisa eat out? _____

_____

4. Does Lisa eat Chinese food when she eats out? _____

_____

Time expressions

A *time expression* tells when something happens. A time expression usually includes one of the following prepositions:

| *in* | *on* | *at* | *from...to* |

Prepositions of time	Example
Use **on** for a specific day or date	I buy food <u>on Mondays</u>.* I buy food <u>on Monday</u>.* I start work <u>on July 5</u>.
Use **in** for the time of day	I exercise <u>in the morning</u>. Juan exercises <u>in the afternoon</u>. Lucy exercises <u>in the evening</u>.
Use **in** for the month, year, or season	My birthday is <u>in July</u>. I was born <u>in 1986</u>. We go skiing <u>in winter</u>.
Use **at** before **night** and for clock time	Lucy exercises <u>at night</u>. Lucy exercises <u>at 6:00</u>.
Use **from...to** for a specific time period	The class is <u>from 9:00 to 10:30</u>.

A time expression can go at the beginning of a sentence or at the end of a sentence. For example, you can say,

I exercise <u>in the morning</u>.

Or you can say,

<u>In the morning,</u> I exercise.

<u>In the morning</u> I exercise.

You can put a comma after time expressions at the beginning of a sentence. It is optional.

Think about it

Work with a partner. Read the paragraph. Put 2 lines under each verb. Put 1 line under each subject. Circle the 7 additional time expressions.

(On Saturday morning,) I usually <u>get up</u> at 9:30. At 10:00, I go to the park to play soccer with my friends. The game is from 10:00 to 11:30. I return home at noon and eat lunch. In the afternoon, I work on my car. In the evening, my wife and I eat out. On Saturday night, we usually watch TV or go to a party.

1. Copy 1 sentence from the paragraph where the time expression is at the beginning of the sentence. _____

2. Copy 1 sentence from the paragraph where the time expression is at the end of the sentence.

_____

* You can say **on Saturday** or **on Saturdays** to refer to something you do every week. Both are correct.

More time expressions

You can also use the prepositions *before* and *after* to talk about when things happen. *Before* and *after* can go at the beginning or end of the sentence. The comma is optional when *before* or *after* are at the beginning of the sentence.

<u>Before class</u> I eat breakfast.   I eat breakfast <u>before class</u>.
<u>Before class</u>, I eat breakfast.

<u>After class</u> I go to work.   I go to work <u>after class</u>.
<u>After class</u>, I go to work.

Think about it

Work with a partner. Read Louisa's schedule. Then complete the sentences using one of the following prepositions: *at*, *in*, *before*, *after*, and *from...to*.

Louisa's schedule	
6:30 a.m.	get up
7:15 a.m.	take a shower
7:45 a.m.	eat breakfast
8:15 a.m.	take the bus to English class
9:00 - 11:45 a.m.	attend English class
12:30 p.m.	take the bus to work
12:30 - 6:30 p.m.	work at the restaurant
7:00 - 8:00 p.m.	go to karate class
8:30 p.m.	walk home and eat dinner
9:15 p.m.	do homework
10:30 p.m.	go to bed

1. Louisa has class <u>**from**</u> 9:00 <u>**to**</u> 12:00.

2. She goes to karate class _____ work.

3. She works _____ the afternoon.

4. _____ 7:45 Louisa eats breakfast.

5. She does homework _____ 9:15 p.m..

6. _____ the morning, she takes a shower.

7. She works _____ 12:30 _____ 6:30.

8. Louisa does homework _____ dinner.

9. She takes a shower _____ breakfast.

10. Louisa goes to karate class _____ 7:00 _____ 8:00.

11. She goes to bed _____ she does her homework.

Talk about it

Ask your partner the following questions. When you answer, use the time expression in parentheses.

1. What time do you get up? (*at*)
2. What day do you wash clothes? (*on*)
3. When is your birthday? (*on*)
4. When do you exercise? (*in* or *at*)
5. What do you do before class? (*before*)
6. When is your class? (*from ___ to ___*)
7. When do you _____?

Practice 4.1: Use the preposition in parentheses to answer the questions. Write complete sentences.

1. What time do you go to bed?

(at) _____

2. What do you do after your class?

(after) _____

3. When do you take a shower?

(in) _____

4. When do you go to class?

(from, to) _____

5. When do you brush your teeth?

(in) _____

6. What do you do before bed?

(before) _____

7. When do you sleep?

(from, to) _____

8. In what month is your birthday?

(in) _____

9. When do you listen to music?

(in) _____

10. What days do you exercise?

(on) _____

Identifying adverbs of frequency

Adverbs of frequency tell how often something happens. Study this table.

		Mon.	Tues.	Wed.	Thur.	Fri.	Sat.	Sun.
I **always** play computer games.	100%							
I **usually** make my bed.								
I **often** go to the mall.								
I **sometimes** eat healthy food.								
I **rarely** take a vacation.								
I **never** go to tattoo parlors.	0%							

The position of adverbs of frequency: the verb *to be*

You often use adverbs of frequency with the verb ***to be*** (***am***, ***is***, and ***are***). Read this sentence.

> My baby is <u>usually</u> hungry.

The adverb of frequency is ***usually.*** It goes *after* the verb ***to be.*** Study the form.

Subject	Verb to be	Adverb of frequency	Rest of sentence
My baby	**is**	**usually**	**hungry.**

These sentences are not correct:

- ~~My baby usually is hungry.~~
- ~~My baby is hungry usually.~~

Think about it

Work with a partner. Read the paragraph out loud. Put 2 lines under each verb. Put 1 line under each subject. Circle the 7 adverbs of frequency. The first sentence is done for you.

<u>My mother</u> <u>is</u> (always) happy. My father is rarely happy. I am usually serious. My sister is always serious. My brother is often funny. My grandmother is sometimes sad.

My grandfather is never sad. Everyone in my family is very different.

Look at the paragraph above. Where are the adverbs of frequency? (Circle the correct answer.)

> a. before the verb ***to be***
> b. after the verb ***to be***
> c. at the beginning of the sentence

Talk about it

Describe yourself to your partner. In each sentence use one of the words in the chart and one adverb of frequency. (For example, *I am often tired*.)

happy	tired	sick
shy	late	lazy
thirsty	sad	hungry
angry	frustrated	bored
kind	busy	generous

Practice 4.2: Put 2 lines under the verb and 1 line under the subject. Then rewrite the sentence using the adverb of frequency.

1. (always) I am tired at night. I am always tired at night.

2. (often) My grandmother is in the hospital. _____

_____

3. (never) The students are lazy._____

_____

4. (rarely) I am late for work. _____

_____

5. (always) My husband is tired after work. _____

_____

6. (usually) Our class is interesting. _____

_____

7. (rarely) My mother's cooking is spicy. _____

_____

8. (often) Tom's boss is annoyed. _____

_____

9. (sometimes) The customers are rude. _____

_____

10. (rarely) I am bored in class. _____

_____

11. (never) Fred is on time. _____

_____

12. (sometimes) We are hungry after class. _____

_____

The position of adverbs of frequency: other verbs

You often use adverbs of frequency with verbs that are not **to be.** Read this sentence.

> I never play soccer.

The adverb of frequency is **never**. It goes *before* the verb when the verb is not **to be**. Here is the form.

Subject	Adverb of frequency	Simple present verb that isn't *to be*	Rest of sentence
I	never	play	soccer.

These sentences are not correct:
- ~~Never I play soccer.~~
- ~~I play soccer never.~~
- ~~I play never soccer.~~

Talk about it

Why are the three sentences above incorrect?

Think about it

Work with a partner. Read the following paragraph out loud. Then:
- Put 2 lines under the verbs.
- Put 1 line under the subject.
- Circle the 10 additional adverbs of frequency.
- Answer the questions.

My wife and I are not healthy eaters. We often eat pasta with lots of butter. We rarely eat vegetables. My wife sometimes eats broccoli. I rarely eat broccoli. We never eat spinach or cauliflower. We always drink coffee and beer. We rarely drink water. Our favorite foods are desserts. I always eat chocolate ice cream. My wife always eats candy. We are always on a diet. We never lose weight.

1. How often does the author eat broccoli? _____

_____

2. How often do the author and his wife eat spinach or cauliflower? _____

_____

3. Is the author on a diet now? _____

_____

Write about it

Work with a partner. Make a sentence. Use the words in parentheses.

- If the verb is **to be**, put the adverb of frequency *after* the verb.
- If the verb is not **to be**, put the adverb of frequency *before* the verb.

1. (sometimes, rainy, New York, is) ___New York is sometimes rainy.___

2. (eats out, my family, rarely) _____

_____

3. (starts, late, often, our class) _____

_____

4. (arrives, at work, on time, rarely, Susanna) _____

_____

5. (visits, my husband, his mother, on Saturdays, usually) _____

_____

6. (babies, hungry, always, are) _____

_____

7. (usually, clothes, on Tuesdays, I, wash) _____

_____

8. (late, stays up, Oliver, on weekends, sometimes) _____

_____

9. (the gym, at, exercise, Fred and Linda, rarely) _____

_____

10. (always, to his son, before bed, Nathan, reads) _____

_____

11. (are, my parents, in Chicago, often) _____

_____

12. (Ana, shy, is, sometimes) _____

_____

13. (often, exercises, Francis, at the gym) _____

_____

14. (never, Luis, on weekends, works) _____

_____

Negative sentences with simple present tense verbs

To make a negative sentence with a simple present tense verb, follow these rules:

- If the sentence includes the verb *to be*, use *am not*, *is not*, *isn't*, *are not*, or *aren't*.

- If the sentence includes a verb that is not *to be*, use *do not*, *don't*, *does not*, or *doesn't* before the base form of the verb.

Use *do not* or *don't* when the subject is *I*, *you*, *we*, or *they* or more than one male, female, or object. Here is the form.

Subject	*do not/don't*	base form	Rest of the sentence
I /We/You/They	do not	work	in the afternoon.
I /We/You/They	don't	work	in the afternoon.

Use *does not* or *doesn't* when the subject is *he*, *she*, *it*, or one male, female, or object. Here is the form.

Subject	*does not/doesn't*	base form	Rest of the sentence
He/She/It	does not	eat	meat.
He/She/It	doesn't	eat	meat.

Study these examples of affirmative and negative sentences.

Simple present affirmative	Simple present negative
They <u>are</u> in the library.	They <u>are</u> **not** in the library. They **aren't** in the library.
Yolanda <u>is</u> from the Philippines.	Yolanda <u>is</u> **not** from the Philippines. Yolanda **isn't** from the Philippines.
I <u>work</u> on Saturday.	I **do not** <u>work</u> on Sunday. I **don't** <u>work</u> on Sunday.
The students <u>study</u> math.	They **do not** <u>study</u> English. They **don't** <u>study</u> English.
Alex <u>works</u> in the afternoon.	Alex **does not** <u>work</u> in the morning. Alex **doesn't** <u>work</u> in the morning.
She <u>has</u> a truck.	She **does not** <u>have</u> a car. She **doesn't** <u>have</u> a car.

Talk about it

Ask your partner the following.

1. Tell me a color you don't like.
2. Tell me a food you don't like.
3. Tell me a language you don't speak.
4. Tell me a kind of music you don't listen to.
5. Tell me one sport you don't watch on TV.

Common mistakes with negative sentences

In negative sentences, use the base verb after *doesn't*.

Incorrect	Correct
Mary doesn't ~~lives~~ here now.	Mary doesn't <u>live</u> here now.

When the subject is *he*, *she*, *it*, or one person or object, use *doesn't*, not *don't*.

Incorrect	Correct
She ~~don't~~ like her job.	She <u>doesn't</u> like her job.

Don't use *no*. Use *not*.

Incorrect	Correct
She ~~no~~ like her job.	She <u>does not</u> like her job.
My parents are ~~no~~ happy in the U.S.	My parents <u>are not</u> happy in the U.S.

Think about it

Work with a partner. One of these sentences is not correct. Cross out the incorrect sentence.

1a. I don't have a job.	1b. ~~I don't has a job.~~
2a. I don't like baseball.	2b. I doesn't like baseball.
3a. Juan no like romantic music.	3b. Juan doesn't like romantic music.
4a. Lily doesn't understand Spanish.	4b. Lily doesn't understands Spanish.
5a. My sister don't work late.	5b. My sister doesn't work late.
6a. I don't remember the answer.	6b. I no remember the answer.
7a. Luis doesn't go to school on Friday.	7b. Luis doesn't goes to school on Friday.
8a. Susanna doesn't has a car.	8b. Susanna doesn't have a car.

Practice 4.3: Make each sentence negative.

1. Luis lives in Tennessee. <u>Luis doesn't live in Tennessee.</u>

2. Maria uses a computer. _____

3. I like my job. _____

4. We are ready. _____

5. Paula studies every day. _____

6. Vincent has a dog. _____

7. Lucy's mother is at work. _____

8. My boss works hard. _____

9. The weather is hot today. _____

10. On weekends we sleep late. _____

Time order words

You use *time order words* to explain the order that events happen. Here are some time order words:

first   next   then   after that   later   finally

The following sentences include time order words. You can put commas after time order words. They are optional.

> <u>First</u> I go to work. <u>After that</u> I go to my class.

> <u>First</u>, I go to work. <u>After that</u>, I go to my class.

Think about it

Look at the sentences above. Where is the time order word?

- a. at the beginning of the sentence
- b. in the middle of the sentence
- c. at the end of the sentence

Talk about it

Tell your partner what you do every morning. Use <u>at least</u> four time order words (***first***, ***next***, ***then***, ***after that***, ***later***, ***finally***).

Practice 4.4: Put 2 lines under each verb. Put 1 line under the subject. Circle the 4 additional time order words. Then answer the questions.

> <u>My Aunt Gloria</u> <u>makes</u> delicious pancakes. (First,) <u>she</u> <u>mixes</u> some flour, baking soda, and salt. Next she adds an egg and some milk. After that she heats the pan. She pours about half a cup of pancake mix into the pan. She cooks the pancake for about three minutes. Then she flips the pancake and cooks it for a few more minutes. Finally, she puts the pancake on a plate.

Read the paragraph again and answer these questions. Use complete sentences.

1. What does Aunt Gloria do first?

_____

2. What does she do after she mixes the flour, baking soda, and salt?

_____

3. What does Gloria do after she flips the pancake?

_____

4. What does she do last?

_____

Talk about it

Work with a partner. Read the sentences. Number the sentences from 1 to 6. Number 1 is the first thing that Irma does and Number 6 is the last thing that she does.

_____ Then she gets dressed. She always wears nice clothes to work.

_____ Finally she is ready for work.

_____ She looks at herself in the mirror again.

_____ After that she irons her clothes.

_____ First she takes a shower, brushes her teeth, and looks in the mirror to put on her makeup.

___1___ Irma gets up at 6:45.

Practice 4.5: Write the sentences above in a paragraph.

Irma gets up at 6:45.

_____

_____

_____

_____

_____

_____

_____

_____

Editing challenge

Now you're ready to practice what you've learned.

- Correct the errors in this paragraph. Each error is underlined.
- Rewrite the paragraph.
- Answer the questions on the next page.

My weekends are quiet. On Saturday morning, I `always sleep late` <u>sleep late always</u>. I often get up <u>10:00.</u> First, I <u>drinks</u> my coffee<u>, I after that</u> clean my apartment. <u>then</u> I give my dog a bath. <u>Always he</u> is very dirty. <u>On the afternoon,</u> my brother and I <u>plays</u> soccer in the <u>Park</u>. Then my brother's wife <u>cook</u> dinner for me. <u>Is</u> always ___ good meal. <u>In the night,</u> I <u>go sometimes</u> to a party at my friend's house. <u>At Sunday in the morning,</u> I go to church. Then I go ____ my house and I <u>does</u> my homework. I <u>no</u> stay up late on <u>sunday</u> night. <u>Always I</u> go to sleep early.

_____ My weekends are quiet. _____

_____

_____

_____

_____

_____

_____

_____

_____

Answer with a complete sentence.

1. What does the author do on Saturday afternoons? _____

   _____

2. Does the author go to bed late on Sunday night? _____

   _____

3. What adverbs of frequency are in this paragraph? _____

   _____

Writing Assignment 4: Preparing to write

For this assignment, you'll write about your weekend. Complete the chart below. Use the verbs below or other verbs. Do not write complete sentences.

go shopping	eat out	watch TV	drive	study
go to church	relax	listen to music	call	clean
go to the gym	exercise	cook (breakfast, lunch, dinner)	play	wash
go to a party	work	do homework	take care of	read
go dancing	do chores	vacuum	sweep	send email

	Morning	**Afternoon**	**Evening**
Saturday	_____ _____	_____ _____	_____ _____
Sunday	_____ _____	_____ _____	_____ _____

Write about it

Write between 7 and 10 sentences about your weekend. Use the information from the chart on the previous page. Do the following:

- Write at least 2 sentences that include time expressions (*On Saturday morning*, *on Sunday night*, *at 2:00*, etc.).

- Write at least 2 sentences that include adverbs of frequency (*always*, *usually*, *often*, *rarely*, *sometimes*, *never*).

- Use at least 3 time order words (*first*, *next*, *then*, *after that*, *later*, *finally*).

- Write at least one negative sentence.

1. _____

2. _____

3. _____

4. _____

5. _____

6. _____

7. _____

8. _____

9. _____

10. _____

Writing Assignment 4: *My Weekend*

Write a paragraph about your weekend.

1. In the top right corner of your paper write:

    Your first and last name

    Today's date

    Assignment 4

2. Indent.

3. Begin the paragraph like this:

    My weekend is usually _____ (*busy*, *quiet*, *active*, *boring*, *good*).

4. Write your paragraph. Write between 7 and 10 sentences. Use the list of sentences above.

5. Skip lines.

6. Start each sentence with a capital letter. End each sentence with a period.

7. Use the editing checklist to check your paragraph. Circle **Yes** or **No** for each item.

Writing Assignment 4: Editing Checklist

Editing Checklist		
Format		
1. My complete name, the date, and the assignment number are in the top right corner of the paper.	Yes	No
2. The first line of the paragraph is indented.	Yes	No
3. The sentences are in a paragraph. They are not in a list.	Yes	No
4. I skipped lines.	Yes	No
Content		
1. All of the sentences are about my weekend.	Yes	No
2. The paragraph has between 7 and 10 sentences.	Yes	No
3. I used at least 3 time expressions (*in*, *on*, etc.).	Yes	No
4. I used at least 3 adverbs of frequency (*always*, *never*, etc.).	Yes	No
5. I used at least 3 time order words (*first*, *then*, etc.).	Yes	No
6. I have 1 negative sentence.	Yes	No
Punctuation and capitalization		
1. I used capital letters correctly.	Yes	No
2. I ended each sentence with a period.	Yes	No
Grammar		
1. Simple present tense verbs that refer to *he*, *she*, or *it* or one person or thing end in an *s*.	Yes	No
2. Each sentence has a subject and a verb.	Yes	No

Chapter 5

Writing About a Picture: Part 1

In this chapter you'll write a paragraph about a picture.

> Luis Martinez
> February 4, 2013
> Assignment 5
>
> "Tonight we're having a party at our house. Everyone in my family is getting ready. My sister is vacuuming the floor. My brother is sweeping the porch. My mother is cleaning the kitchen. My father is in the kitchen making food. And I'm relaxing. I'm waiting for someone to say, "Luis, start helping.""

Answer each question with a complete sentence.

1. What is Luis's sister doing? _____

_____

2. Where is Luis's father? _____

_____

3. Is Luis helping? _____

_____

4. Where is the party? _____

_____

Present continuous verbs

You use *present continuous* verbs to talk about what is happening right now. Read this sentence:

- I am driving to work now.

The subject is *I*. The verb is **am driving**. This verb has two parts:

- **am** is the *auxiliary* verb.

- **driving** is the *base verb* plus **ing**. This verb form is called the *present participle*.

A complete sentence in the present progressive tense must include both the auxiliary verb and the main verb. Also, the main verb must end in **ing**. This is the form.

Subject	Auxiliary verb (Verb **to be**)	Main verb (Base Verb + **ing**)	Rest of the sentence
I	am	driving	now.

Think about it

Work with a partner. Put two lines under the present continuous verb. Then put one line under the subject.

1. I am working now.

2. My teacher is taking a break.

3. Juan and Ernesto are exercising at the gym.

4. The employees are wearing their uniforms.

5. Today my uncle is playing soccer with my father.

6. The nurses are working overtime today.

7. Right now Juan is doing his homework.

8. Cecilia is playing basketball at the park.

9. My parents are driving to Los Angeles.

10. The customers are waiting in line.

11. Ben and Mario are fixing their car.

12. My aunt is swimming in the pool at the park.

Practice 5.1: Write each sentence using a present continuous verb. If you don't know how to spell present continuous verbs, see Appendix A.

1. (read) Peter_____*is reading*_____ a story to his daughter.

2. (play) Jessica _____ the piano.

3. (take) The students _____ a test.

4. (make) Ana _____ dinner.

5. (help) The children _____ their teacher.

6. (watch) My friends _____ soccer on TV.

7. (clean) Daniel and I _____ the kitchen.

8. (do) Nisha _____ the laundry.

9. (meet) I _____ with my boss.

10. (bake) My mother_____ a cake for my husband's birthday.

11. (take) The woman in the green car _____ my parking space.

12. (put) Angela _____ away her clothes.

13. (sit) The boys _____ quietly.

14. (get) My son _____dressed for school.

15. (practice) The students _____ their English.

16. (exercise) I _____ at the gym.

17. (visit) Maria, Martina, and Lily _____ their aunt in Fresno.

18. (do) Right now, my husband _____ the dishes.

19. (smile) The people in the photo _____

20. (take care of) Ryan _____Jack.

Talk about it

Ask your partner questions about the people in the pictures below. Ask one of these questions.

- What is he doing?
- What is she doing?
- What are they doing?

Partner B replies using one of the verbs in the box below.

dance	drive	run	eat
drink	clean	read	watch
walk	hold	plant	build

Common mistakes with present continuous verbs

Present continuous verbs must include the verb *to be*.

Incorrect	Correct
I ~~working~~.	I am working.

Present continuous verbs must include a base verb with *ing*.

Incorrect	Correct
I am ~~work~~.	I am working.

Practice 5.2: Read each sentence.

- If the sentence is correct, put an X in the *Correct* box.
- If the sentence is incorrect,
    - Put an X in the *Incorrec*t box.
    - In the *Problem* box, write **no auxiliary verb** or **no ing verb.**
    - Correct the sentence.

	Correct	Incorrect	Problem
1. My sister is ~~work~~ working now.		X	no ing verb
2. I am playing soccer.			
3. My parents are watch TV.			
4. Jose is drive to work.			
5. My sister going to school.			
6. The children are sleeping.			
7. We listening to music.			
8. Anita and Ana are work in Dallas.			
9. My boss is studying Chinese.			
10. The sun is shine today.			
11. That child doing her homework.			
12. I am working late today.			

Write about it

Work with a partner. Write 5 additional sentences that use present continuous verbs. Use words from each column. Use each main verb once.

Subject	Auxiliary verb	Main verb
Angelica	am	walking
Mario	is	talking
I	are	reading
The students		studying
My friend		driving
Jacob and I		working

1. <u>Angelica is playing soccer.</u>

2. _____

3. _____

4. _____

5. _____

6. _____

Practice 5.3: There are a total of 5 verb errors in each paragraph. Correct the errors.

Paragraph 1

    Many people are working at Pop's Pizza. Mr. Wilson is ~~take~~ ^{taking} orders. Jose and Mario is making pizza. Leslie is serving pizza. Roger is make salad. Miguel washing the dishes. Luz is working at the cash register. Maria clearing the tables.

Paragraph 2

    It is a beautiful day at the park. Ana, Alex and Sonia are playing soccer. Lucas is play soccer too. Laura and Dulce talking. Jorge is read the newspaper. Some children swimming. The birds is singing. The sun is shining.

Paragraph 3

The classroom is very busy. Arturo taking a test. Luis is writing an essay. Jessica and Amanda studying vocabulary words. Lupita is reading her textbook. Jorge and Angela is practicing a conversation. Maribel and Jonathan is erasing the board. The teacher is help a student.

Punctuation

Punctuation makes sentences easy to understand. These are some punctuation marks in English:

- period (.)
- comma (,)
- question mark (?)

Think about it

Read this paragraph. Then answer the questions.

Disneyland is the most famous amusement park in the United States. More than 40,000 people visit Disneyland every day. It has 36 rides. Some popular rides are Space Mountain, Indiana Jones, and Splash Mountain. I want to visit Disneyland. Do you?

1. How many question marks are in this paragraph? _____

2. How many commas are in this paragraph? _____

3. How many periods are in this paragraph? _____

4. What are three punctuation marks in English? _____

_____

Run-on sentences

Read this sentence.

I am cooking my dog is eating.

This is an example of a *run-on sentence*. A *run-on sentence* is a long sentence that is difficult to understand. A run-on sentence usually can be divided into two sentences. Look at these examples of run-on sentences. Then look at the correction.

Run-on sentence:	~~I am cooking my dog is eating.~~
Problem:	There is no period at the end of the first sentence. There is no capital letter at the beginning of the second sentence.
Correction:	**I am cooking. My dog is eating.**

Run-on sentence:	~~I am cooking, my dog is eating.~~
Problem:	There is a comma at the end of the first sentence. There is no period at the end of the first sentence. The second sentence doesn't begin with a capital letter.
Correction:	**I am cooking. My dog is eating.**

Think about it

Work with a partner. Correct these sentences so they are not run-on sentences.

1. I have two brothers~~, they~~. They live in Dallas.

2. We are walking our dog is sleeping.

3. San Carlos is a small city my city is much bigger.

4. The stores at the mall are expensive, I like the flea market.

5. On Tuesday, Adam goes to ESL class, then he goes to work.

6. Jose works late on Tuesdays, Gabriela works late on Thursdays.

7. John is eating Martha is not hungry.

8. I need to buy milk, I need to go to the bank, after that I need to pick up my daughter.

Practice 5.4: Each paragraph has 3 run-on sentences. Correct them.

Paragraph 1

Right now I am cooking my husband is cleaning. My son is washing his car. My daughter is at the gym, her husband is with her. The dog is sleeping on Monday we all go back to work.

Paragraph 2

Coke is not good for you one can of Coke has 10 teaspoons of sugar. Many people drink four or five cans of Coke a day. Drinking Coke can make you fat, it also is bad for your body. I let my children have one Coke every week they are angry. I want them to be healthy.

Paragraph 3

Facebook is very popular, it also is fun. People like to share photos they like to tell about their life. Some people have more than 500 Facebook friends. Facebook is a good way to communicate with people in other countries in my opinion you can waste a lot of time on Facebook.

Editing challenge

Now you're ready to practice what you've learned.

- Look at the picture and read the paragraph about the picture.
- Correct the errors in this paragraph. Each error is underlined.
- Rewrite the paragraph.
- Answer the questions.

It is a beautiful day at <u>paradise beach</u>. A boy is playing in the sand<u>,</u> <u>a</u> dog

is <u>play</u> too<u>, a</u> lady <u>drinking</u> a <u>coke</u>. In the ocean, a man is <u>catch</u> a fish. Another man

<u>selling</u> ice cream. Two boys are <u>plaYing</u> catch with a ball. <u>Everyone</u> happy. <u>Is</u> hot. The

<u>sky blue</u>.

It is a beautiful day at

_____

_____

_____

_____

_____

_____

_____

_____

1. What is the man selling? _____

_____

2. What is the weather at the beach? _____

_____

3. Where are the people? _____

_____

4. Write three sentences in the paragraph that have present continuous verbs.

a. _____

b. _____

c. _____

Writing Assignment 5: Preparing to write

Talk about it

Work with a partner. Look at the drawing. Point to each of these words.

1. bench	5. path
2. pond	6. jump rope
3. kite	7. grass
4. cane	8. hill

Think about it

Work with a partner. Look at the drawing. Write 6 more present participles (*ing* verbs) that describe what the people are doing.

1. chasing	6. _____
2. rollerblading	7. _____
3. flying (a kite)	8. _____
4. jumping (rope)_	9. _____
5. _____	10. _____

Write about it

Write between 7 and 10 sentences about the picture on the previous page. Use the nouns and verbs in the boxes on the previous page.

1. _____

2. _____

3. _____

4. _____

5. _____

6. _____

7. _____

8. _____

9. _____

10. _____

Writing Assignment 5: Write about a picture

Write a paragraph about the picture on the previous page. Follow these steps:

1. In the top right corner of your paper write:

>   Your first and last name

>   Today's date

>   **Assignment 5**

2. Indent and begin the paragraph like this:

>   It is a busy day at the park.

3. Skip lines.

4. <u>Write between 7 and 10 more sentences. Use the sentences you wrote above.</u>

5. Use the editing checklist to check your work. Circle **Yes** or **No** for each item in the checklist.

Writing Assignment 5: Editing Checklist

Editing Checklist		
Format		
1. My complete name, the date, and the assignment number are in the top right corner of the paper.	Yes	No
2. The first line is indented.	Yes	No
3. Sentences are in a paragraph. They are not in a list.	Yes	No
4. I skipped lines.	Yes	No
Content		
1. My paragraph has between 7 and 10 sentences.	Yes	No
2. All of the sentences are about the picture.	Yes	No
Capitalization and punctuation		
1. I used capital letters correctly.	Yes	No
2. Each sentence ends with a period.	Yes	No
Grammar		
1. Sentences with present continuous verbs have an auxiliary verb and a main verb that ends in *ing*.	Yes	No
2. All sentences have a subject and a verb.	Yes	No
3. There are no run-on sentences.	Yes	No

Chapter 6

Writing About a Picture: Part 2

In this chapter you'll write another paragraph about a picture.

Raymundo Chavez
February 7, 2013
Assignment 6

It is Saturday night and the Fox Theater is crowded. Many people are waiting in line. At the ticket window, a man is selling tickets. Another man is collecting tickets. A mother and her daughter are buying popcorn and soda. Inside the theatre, people are talking to their friends. They are waiting for the movie to begin. Then it is dark. The movie is starting.

Answer each question with a complete sentence.

1. What day of the week is it? _____

_____

2. Where are the people? _____

_____

3. What is the mother buying? _____

_____

4. What is the man collecting? _____

_____

More about subject pronouns

A *subject pronoun* is a word that replaces the subject of a sentence. **I**, **you**, **he**, **she**, **it**, **we**, and **they** are all subject pronouns. Read this paragraph. In many of the sentences, subject pronouns are not used correctly.

> Ana Chan is an excellent artist. Paints many beautiful pictures. He uses special paints. Ana she sometimes draws with special pencils. Sells her pictures for a lot of money.

Here is the same paragraph with pronouns used correctly.

> Ana Chan is an excellent artist. She paints many beautiful pictures. She uses special paints. She sometimes draws with special pencils. She sells her pictures for a lot of money.

Talk about it

Why is the second paragraph clearer than the first paragraph?

Common mistakes with subject pronouns

These are three common mistakes with pronouns.

No subject: Every sentence must have a subject. Sometimes the subject is a pronoun.

Incorrect	Correct
Angela is a student. ~~Goes~~ to Sequoia Adult School.	Angela is a student. <u>She</u> goes to Sequoia Adult School.
Today is July 22. ~~Is~~ my birthday.	Today is July 22. <u>It</u> is my birthday.

Redundant subject: Do not use both a noun and pronoun for the same subject.

Incorrect	Correct
~~Angela she~~ is a student.	<u>Angela</u> is a student.
	or
	<u>She</u> is a student.

Incorrect pronoun: The pronoun must refer to the correct noun.

Incorrect	Correct
Angela is a student. ~~He~~ goes to Sequoia Adult School.	Angela is a student. <u>She</u> goes to Sequoia Adult School.
My parents are great people. ~~He~~ help me a lot.	My parents are great people. <u>They</u> help me a lot

Think about it

Work with a partner.

- Read each sentence.

- If the sentence is correct, put an *X* in the *Correct* column.

- If the sentence is incorrect, put an *X* in the *Incorrect* column and correct the error.

	Correct	Incorrect
She 1. Maria is a good person. ~~He~~ is from Guatemala.		X
2. My parents they don't like the United States.		
3. My daughter she is sick today.		
4. My father works hard. Is a janitor in a big building.		
5. That student she misses class every day.		
6. The class is boring. She is not interesting.		
7. The doctors are busy. He have many patients.		
8. My teacher likes her job.		
9. It is 9:00. Is very late.		
10. I see the keys. They are on the table.		
11. My cell phone is old. Needs a new battery.		
12. My aunt is sick. He needs to go to the doctor.		
13. Calico she is a good cat.		
14. The cupcakes are chocolate. They are delicious.		

When to use nouns and when to use pronouns

Read this paragraph.

> She is beautiful. She is kind and generous. She is talented. She is rich. I want to marry her.

Who is *she*? We don't know. Now read this.

> Penelope Cruz is beautiful. She is kind and generous. She is talented. She is rich. I want to marry her.

This paragraph is clear. The writer is talking about Penelope Cruz!

Think about it

Look at this photo. Then read the two paragraphs below. Answer the question.

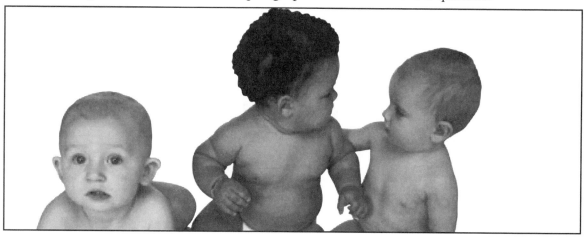

Paragraph 1

> His name is Sam. He is six months old. His name is Jack. He is seven months old. He is Martin. He is also seven months old.

Paragraph 2

> The baby on the left is Sam. He is six months old. The baby in the middle is Jack. He is seven months old. The baby on the right is Martin. He is also seven months old.

Which paragraph is clearer? Why? _____

_____

Practice 6.1: Read the paragraph about the picture. Replace each underlined pronoun with a noun. Use the words in the box.

A waiter	A busser	A waitress
A father	A mother	

It is lunchtime at the restaurant. <u>She</u> is carrying a tray of food. <u>He</u> is clearing the table. <u>He</u> is taking an order. <u>She</u> is giving a piece of cake to her daughter. <u>He</u> is pouring water.

It is lunchtime at the restaurant. A

waitress is

Verbs followed by prepositions

A *preposition* is a word, often a short word, that tells about time or location. Examples of prepositions are **in**, **on**, **at**, **to**, *and* **for**. Some verbs are often followed by specific prepositions. For example, **listen** is usually followed by **to**. This sentence is correct.

> I am listening to music now.

This sentence is not correct.

> I ~~am listening~~ music now.

Think about it

Work with a partner. Write the correct verb + preposition under the picture.

| paying for | listening to | looking for |
| waiting for | waking up | looking at |

_____

_____

_____

_____

_____

_____

Talk about it

Ask your partner about each drawing. Ask **What is he doing?** or **What is she doing?** Use a verb + preposition in every response.

Practice 6.2:. Use a verb + preposition from the pictures above to complete each sentence. Use present continuous verbs.

1. Han ___is looking at___ his watch because he is late.

2. The students _____ music at their class party.

3. It is 6:00 a.m. My son _____ early today.

4. Susan _____ her keys again. She loses them every day.

5. I _____ the bus. It's late again.

6. My parents _____ our tickets to the movie.

Using *and* or *or* to connect words

Read these sentences.

> Joe wants a hotdog. Joe wants a hamburger. Joe wants fries.

Use *and* to make these sentences into one sentence.

> Joe wants a hotdog, a hamburger, **and** fries.

If you use *or*, the sentence has a different meaning. It means that Joe only wants one kind of food.

> Joe wants a hotdog, a hamburger, **or** fries.

Use *and* or *or* to connect subjects.

> <u>Bob</u> **and** <u>Henry</u> can work tomorrow.
> <u>Bob</u> **or** <u>Henry</u> can work tomorrow.

Use *and* or *or* to connect verbs.

> My daughter <u>washes</u> **and** <u>dries</u> the dishes every day.
> My daughter <u>washes</u> **or** <u>dries</u> the dishes every day.

Use *and* or *or* to connect words after the verb.

> You need to buy <u>Coke, Fanta,</u> **and** <u>Sprite.</u>
> You need to buy <u>Coke, Fanta,</u> **or** <u>Sprite.</u>

Talk about it.

1. Read this sentence.

> Mario wants a toy car, a toy truck, and a toy soldier.

How many toys does Mario want? _____

2. Read this sentence.

> Mario wants a toy car, a toy truck, or a toy soldier.

How many toys does Mario want? _____

Talk about it

Ask your partner these questions. Use *and* in every answer. Use only one sentence in your answer. Remember to use simple present tense verbs.

1. What are three things you do every morning?
2. What are three things you do every evening?
3. What are three things you usually do on Saturdays?
4. What are three places you want to visit?
5. Name three things you like about the United States.
6. Name three things you don't like about the United States.

Using commas with *and* and *or*

When a sentence has three or more items, put a comma after each item except the last item. For example,

We need <u>eggs, milk, and butter</u>. We don't need <u>apples, bread, or onions</u>.

When a sentence has two items, don't use a comma. For example,

We need <u>eggs and butter</u>. We don't need <u>apples or onions</u>.

The comma in these sentences is *not* correct.

We need ~~eggs,~~ and butter. We don't need ~~apples,~~ or onions.

Do not use more than one **and** or **or** in the same list. Only use **and** or **or** before the last item. These sentences are *not* correct.

We need eggs, ~~and~~ milk, and butter. We don't need apples, ~~or~~ bread, or onions.

Think about it

* Read the sentences in the chart.

* If the sentence is correct, put an X in the *Correct* box.

* If the sentence is incorrect, put an X in the *Incorrect* box and correct the error.

	Correct	Incorrect
1. We can have pizza, pasta, or chicken for dinner.		X
2. They play soccer basketball and baseball on Saturdays.		
3. I want to visit New York, or Boston.		
4. Louisa, Ana, Bob, and Gladys are studying in the library.		
5. You can ride your bicycle walk or take the train.		
6. I want to be an engineer, a nurse, or a doctor.		
7. Ning can work on Monday Tuesday, or Friday.		
8. My sister and my uncle and my aunt are at home now.		
9. Mario, Phil or John can work on Wednesday.		
10. I need to wash clothes iron and do the dishes.		

Practice 6.3: Combine two sentences into one sentence. Use **and** or **or**. In some sentences, you may need to change the verb.

1. **and** (Ellen is making dinner. Patricia is making dinner.) Ellen and Patricia are making dinner._____

2. **and** (Agnes is at home. Roberto is at home. Juliet is at home.)_____

_____

3. **or** (You need to buy apple juice. You need to buy orange juice.) _____

_____

4. **and** (I am working. I am studying.) _____

_____

5. **and** (Lisa needs to sweep the floor. Joe needs to sweep the floor. Ben needs to sweep the floor.) _____

6. **and** (Angela is working. Mario is working. Luis is working.) _____

_____

7. **and** (Your shoes are on the floor. Your keys are on the floor. Your clothes are on the floor.)

_____

8. **or** (We can visit New York. We can visit Boston.) _____

_____

9. **and** (My girlfriend is beautiful. My girlfriend is hardworking. My girlfriend is romantic.)

_____

10. **or** (We can play football. We can play baseball. We can play volleyball.) _____

_____

Practice 6.4: Answer the questions with one sentence. Use **and** to connect words.

1. What are your three favorite fruits? _____

_____

2. What are your two favorite vegetables? _____

_____

3. What are three things you usually do on Sundays? _____

_____

4. Name three people sitting near you. _____

_____

Topic sentences

The *topic sentence* tells what a paragraph is about. It is the main idea. The topic sentence is usually the first sentence in the paragraph. Read this paragraph.

> My favorite color is blue. I love to be outside and the sky outside is blue. I like to swim in the ocean and the ocean is blue too. My favorite food is blueberries. Of course, blueberries are also blue. But I don't like blue hair.

The topic sentence is My favorite color is blue. That is also the main idea of the paragraph.

Think about it

- Read each paragraph below.
- Underline the topic sentence.
- Answer the question by circling the correct letter.

Paragraph 1

> My family is usually lazy on Saturdays. Right now my husband is sitting on the couch. He is watching football on TV and drinking a soda. My son is sleeping. My daughter is reading a magazine. I am texting my friend. My dog wants to go outside, but everyone is too lazy to open the door.

What is the main idea of this paragraph?
  A. The author's husband likes football.
  B. The author's family is lazy on Saturdays.
  C. The author likes to text.
  D. The author has a cell phone.

Paragraph 2

> My baby niece Louisa is usually happy. She likes to eat bananas, cereal, and Cheerios. Louisa doesn't like her car seat. In the car seat, Louisa cries and cries. When she is not in the car seat, she is a very happy baby.

What is the main idea of this paragraph?

  A. Louisa is usually a happy baby.
  B. Louisa likes to eat bananas.
  C. Louisa cries a lot.
  D. Louisa cries in her car seat.

Paragraph 3

Running is good exercise. It has many advantages. You can run outside and enjoy the sun. You don't need special clothes. You don't need to go to a gym. Running has disadvantages too. It can cause knee problems and ankle problems. If the weather is cold, it is difficult to run outside.

What is the main idea of this paragraph?
   A. Running is important.
   B. Running in cold weather is difficult.
   C. There are good and bad things about running.
   D. Exercise is important.

Paragraph 4

The largest animal in the world is the blue whale. About one hundred people can fit in a blue whale's mouth. A blue whale's heart weighs 1,300 pounds. When a blue whale is born, it can weigh 6,000 pounds.

What is the main idea of this paragraph?
   A. Blue whales are very big.
   B. A blue whale has a very big mouth.
   C. Blue whales have big babies.
   D. A blue whale has a big heart.

Think about it

- Read each paragraph.
- Choose the best topic sentence.
- Write the topic sentence on the line.

Paragraph 1

_____In high school he played basketball and soccer. He was the captain of both teams. When Vinnie was in high school, his teams won the state championship. Now Vinnie plays basketball in college. He wants to be a professional basketball player.

Choose the best topic sentence. Write it on the line above.
   A. Basketball is a great sport.
   B. Sports are very important in high school.
   C. Vinnie is a great athlete.
   D. Vinnie is my friend.

Paragraph 2

_____I have
four children. They make a lot of noise. My wife likes loud music. My dog often barks,
especially when it is scared. I can't sleep because my house is so noisy.

Choose the best topic sentence. Write it on the line above.

    A. My children are not quiet.

    B. My street is noisy.

    C. My house is very noisy.

    D. My family is wonderful.

Paragraph 3

_____Many patients
are waiting in the waiting room. There are children and adults. Some people are
sneezing and coughing. The receptionist is helping patients fill out forms. The doctors
and nurses are examining the patients.

Choose the best topic sentence. Write it on the line above.

    A. The doctor's office is busy today.

    B. The doctors need help.

    C. The doctor's office needs more chairs.

    D. I feel sick today.

Paragraph 4

_____You need
four things: the correct temperature, sun, water, and a place to plant your vegetables.
Some vegetables, such as tomatoes and squash, need warm weather to grow. Other
vegetables, like lettuce, can grow in cooler weather. If you don't have a yard, you can
grow vegetables in pots. You need to water your vegetables every day or every two
days.

Choose the best topic sentence. Write it on the line above.

    A. Tomatoes need hot weather to grow.

    B. Vegetables need water.

    C. It's easy to grow vegetables.

    D. Vegetables are delicious.

Editing challenge

You have learned several editing skills. Now you're going to use them!

- Look at the picture and read the paragraph.
- Correct the errors. Each error is underlined.
- Rewrite the paragraph.
- Answer the questions on the next page.

    Many people are <u>eat</u> lunch at the <u>blue moon,</u> the <u>waiter he</u> is taking an order. <u>the</u> lady <u>holding</u> her menu. <u>Her</u> is also <u>talk</u> to the waiter. A busser is setting the table<u>_he</u> is very <u>Busy</u>. The <u>waitress she</u> is carrying <u>plates glasses</u> and <u>bowl</u> to the customers. <u>Is busy</u> also. A <u>mother father</u> and child are <u>eat</u> lunch at the <u>Restaurant</u>.

_____

_____

_____

_____

_____

_____

_____

_____

1. What is the name of the restaurant? _____

_____

2. What meal are the people eating? _____

_____

3. What is the waitress doing? _____

_____

Writing Assignment 6: Preparing to write

For this assignment you will write about the picture below.

Think about it

Work with a partner. Look at the picture. Write verbs that describe what people in the picture are doing. Use some of the verbs followed by prepositions you learned earlier in this chapter.

1. _____   5. _____

2. _____   6. _____

3. _____   7. _____

4. _____   8. _____

Write about it

- Write between 7 and 10 sentences about the picture on the previous page. Use the verbs in the box on the previous page.

- Include **_and_** in at least 1 sentence.

1. _____

2. _____

3. _____

4. _____

5. _____

6. _____

7. _____

8. _____

9. _____

10. _____

Writing Assignment 6: Write about a picture

Write a paragraph about the picture on the previous page. Follow these steps:

1. In the top right corner of your paper write the *heading*. The heading includes:

    Your first and last name

    Today's date

    Assignment 6

2. Indent. Then write one of these topic sentences:

    The train station is very busy.

    It is a busy day at the train station.

    Many people are waiting for the train.

4. Write between 7 and 10 sentences. Copy the sentences you wrote above.

5. Use the editing checklist on the next page to check your work. Circle **Yes** or **No** for each item in the checklist.

Writing Assignment 6: Editing Checklist

Editing Checklist		
Format		
1. I have a correct heading.	Yes	No
2. The first line is indented.	Yes	No
3. I skipped lines.	Yes	No
Content		
1. The paragraph has a topic sentence.	Yes	Yes
2. My paragraph has between 7 and 10 sentences.	Yes	No
3. I used *and* in at least 1 sentence.	Yes	No
Capitalization and punctuation		
1. I used capital letters correctly.	Yes	No
2. I ended each sentence with a period.	Yes	No
Grammar		
1. Present continuous verbs have an auxiliary verb and a main verb that ends in *ing*.	Yes	No
2. All sentences have a subject and a verb.	Yes	No
3. I used pronouns correctly.	Yes	No
4. There are no run-on sentences.	Yes	No

Chapter 7

A Special Person

In this chapter you'll write about a special person.

Patty Hernandez
Feb. 11, 2013
Assignment 7

My great grandmother is a special person. She is energetic. She walks three miles every day, and she only sleeps for seven hours every night. She is hardworking. She often cleans our house and washes the dishes. She is intelligent too. She doesn't speak English, but she understands everything. She is thoughtful. She always bakes birthday cakes for my siblings and me. But she doesn't celebrate her own birthday. I think she is 94 years old, but I'm not sure.

Answer each question with a complete sentence.

1. Who is this paragraph about? _____

_____

2. How far does Patty's great grandmother walk each day? _____

_____

3. Does Patty's great grandmother speak English? _____

_____

4. How old is Patty's great grandmother?_____

_____

Identifying adjectives

An *adjective* is a word that describes a noun or pronoun. Adjectives can describe what people look like. Examples are **tall**, **short**, **heavy**, and **thin**. Adjectives can describe how people feel. Examples are **happy** and **tired**. Adjectives can describe size and color. Examples are **big**, **small**, **red**, and **yellow**. Here are examples of adjectives used with the verb **to be**.

- My uncle is <u>heavy</u>.

- Ana's eyes are <u>blue</u>.

Building your vocabulary: adjectives

Adjectives can describe a person's appearance. Here are some examples. Words next to the slash (/) symbol mean the same thing. For example, **heavy** and **overweight** mean the same thing.

_____	heavy/overweight	_____	beautiful/gorgeous	_____	dark
_____	thin/skinny/slim	_____	pretty	_____	fair
_____	tall	_____	handsome	_____	bald
_____	short	_____	ugly	_____	petite
_____	curly (hair)	_____	cute	_____	muscular
_____	wavy (hair)	_____	old	_____	well-dressed/fashionable
_____	straight (hair)	_____	middle-aged	_____	tattooed
_____	blue, green, black (eyes)	_____	young	_____	unkempt

Talk about it

- Read the adjectives in the box above. Put a check next to each adjective you know.
- Learn the meanings of adjectives you don't know. Ask your classmates or find the definition in a dictionary.

Write about it

Write three adjectives you just learned. Use each adjective in a sentence.

Adjective	Sentence with that adjective
1.	
2.	
3.	

Adjectives describe a person's character. Here are some examples. Words next to the / symbol mean the same thing.

_____ nice/kind	_____ friendly	_____ curious
_____ mean	_____ unfriendly	_____ helpful
_____ talkative	_____ nervous	_____ talented
_____ quiet/shy	_____ calm	_____ generous
_____ lazy	_____ active	_____ selfish
_____ hardworking/industrious	_____ studious	_____ compassionate
_____ serious	_____ intelligent/smart	_____ organized
_____ funny	_____ stupid/dumb	_____ disorganized
_____ mature	_____ silly	_____ thoughtful/considerate
_____ immature	_____ polite	_____ inconsiderate
_____ responsible	_____ disagreeable	_____ successful
_____ irresponsible	_____ agreeable	_____ aggressive

Talk about it

- Read the adjectives in the box above. Put a check next to each adjective you know.
- Learn the meanings of adjectives you don't know. Ask your classmates or find the definition in a dictionary.

Write about it

Write 5 adjectives you just learned. Use each adjective in a sentence.

Adjective	Sentence with that adjective
1.	
2.	
3.	
4.	
5.	

Using more than one adjective in a sentence

You can use multiple adjectives in a sentence. It is fine to say,

> My boyfriend is handsome. He is intelligent. He is studious.

But it is better to say,

> My boyfriend is handsome, intelligent, and studious.

Talk about it

Tell your partner:

- Describe your best friend. Use at least four adjectives. Use one sentence.

- Describe your sister or mother. Use at least four adjectives. Use one sentence.

- Describe your brother or father. Use at least four adjectives. Use one sentence.

- Describe yourself. Use at least four adjectives. Use one sentence.

- Describe your partner. Use at least four adjectives. Use one sentence.

The position of adjectives

An adjective can follow the verb **to be**. For example

- Amanda is <u>sick</u>.

The adjective, **sick**, comes after the verb **is**.

You can also put the adjective *before* the noun it describes. Read this sentence.

- My <u>beautiful</u> girlfriend is my <u>favorite</u> person in the world.

Notice the following:

- The adjective **beautiful** comes before the noun **girlfriend**.

- The adjective **favorite** comes before the noun **person**.

Think about it

Work with a partner. Circle all of the adjectives in this paragraph. There are a total of 12. Numbers are adjectives. The first adjective is circled.

My brother is handsome. He has curly hair and dark eyes. He is tall and slender. He is also very muscular. He goes to the gym every day. He works at the gym too. He is a trainer. He is hardworking and successful. He has 15 clients. He is talkative and funny. His clients are happy when they exercise.

Practice 7.1

- Put 2 lines under the verb.
- Put 1 line under the subject.
- Circle each adjective. Some sentences have more than one adjective.

1. I need (new) shoes.

2. The blue pencil is on the floor.

3. Ben lives in a dangerous neighborhood.

4. My parents have a huge vegetable garden with tomatoes, squash, and basil.

5. My generous boss often gives me a big raise.

6. The weather is hot and sunny today.

7. Our inconsiderate neighbors often play loud music.

8. My studious cousin is at the library.

9. Hoover Park has a small lake, beautiful trees, and a large pool.

10. Laura lives in a big, old house.

Common mistakes with adjectives

Adjectives are never plural.

Incorrect	Correct
The books are news.	The books are new.

Adjectives go before the noun they describe.

Incorrect	Correct
My sister has hair short.	My sister has short hair.

Use **an** before an adjective that starts with a vowel.

Incorrect	Correct
You have a interesting job.	You have an interesting job.

Do not use **color** to describe colors.

Incorrect	Correct
I like your shoes color red.	I like your red shoes.

Think about it

Work with a partner. Cross out the incorrect sentence.

1a. ~~My sister has a job new.~~	1b. My sister has a new job.
2a. I have a car old.	2b. I have an old car.
3a. My wonderful brother always makes delicious food for our family.	3b. My wonderful brother always makes food delicious for our family.
4a. My gray pants are dirty.	4b. My pants gray are dirty.
5a. Those are beautiful flowers.	5b. Those are beautifuls flowers.
6a. It is hot today.	6b. Is hot today.
7a. The students Chinese are from Beijing.	7b. The Chinese students are from Beijing.
8a. Alma has hair color black and eyes color blue.	8b. Alma has black hair and blue eyes.
9a. My cat has an easy life.	9b. My cat has a easy life.
10a. San Francisco is a exciting city.	10b. San Francisco is an exciting city.
11a. The students are talented.	11b. The students are talenteds.
12a. I have a wonderful boss.	12b. I have an wonderful boss.
13a. Be careful of the glass broken.	13b. Be careful of the broken glass.
14a. That restaurant Italian is delicious.	14b. That Italian restaurant is delicious.

Practice 7.2: Read each sentence.

- If the sentence is correct, put an X in the *Correct* box.

- If the sentence is not correct, put an X in the *Incorrect* box. Then correct the sentence.

	Correct	Incorrect
1. We have a ~~cat new~~. _{new cat}		X
2. Your gold earrings are beautiful.		
3. The students are lates.		
4. Lance always buys milk organic and fruit fresh.		
5. The new house is in a nice neighborhood.		
6. She has hair color brown.		
7. The weather today is sunny and warm.		
8. We have a interesting class with many students good.		
9. The pizzas are colds and the beer is warm.		
10. The paint red is on the table.		

Using *and* and *but* to connect sentences

You already know how to write a *simple sentence*. A simple sentences has this form.

Subject	Verb	Rest of the sentence
Angelica	lives	in Houston.
Angelica	lives and works	in Houston.
Angelica and Ryan	live	in Houston.
Angelic and Ryan	live and work	in Houston.

A *compound* sentence joins two *clauses*. A *clause* has a subject and a verb. The clauses in a compound sentence are connected by a *conjunction*. Two common conjunctions are *and* and *but*.

Use *and* to connect two clauses that have similar ideas. A compound sentence with *and* has this form.

Subject	Verb	Rest of the sentence		Subject	Verb	Rest of the sentence
My mother	likes	to cook,	**and**	I	like	her food.

Use *but* to connect two clauses with ideas that are different or surprising. A compound sentence with *but* has this form.

Subject	Verb	Rest of the sentence		Subject	Verb	Rest of the sentence
My mother	likes	to cook,	**but**	I	don't like	her food.

Notice the following:

A compound sentence has two *clauses* or parts. The two parts are joined by a conjunction such as *and* or *but*.
- Each clause is a complete sentence. It has a subject and a verb.

- In a compound sentence, use a comma immediately before the conjunctions *and* and *but*.

Think about it

Work with a partner. Read each compound sentence out loud.

- Put two lines under the verb in each clause.
- Put one line under the subject in each clause.
- Put a circle around the conjunction that joins the two clauses.

1. Jessica has two jobs, and she is also a student.

2. My daughter lives in Redwood City, but she goes to school in San Mateo.

3. My computer is new, but it is often broken.

4. My daughter is five years old, and my son is six years old.

5. I always remember my notebook, and I forget my pen.

6. Victor is only five years old, but he can read.

7. The students often arrive late, and they leave early.

8. Arnold and Ng usually work late on Tuesdays, and Julie and I work late on Wednesdays.

9. My sister and brother-in-law live in Colorado, and I visit them once a year.

10. We elect a president and vice-president every four years, but I can't vote.

11. Ana and Ricky are married, but they don't have children.

12. My sister plays soccer every week, and her husband plays basketball three times a week.

13. Before class Fred, Jack, and Alice clean the tables, and Shen and Marcos erase the whiteboard.

14. Kai studies English, and I study Chinese.

15. On Wednesdays I go to school at night, and my husband takes care of our children.

Think about it

Read the paragraph.

- Underline each verb with two lines.
- Underline each subject with one line.
- Put a circle around each conjunction (*and* or *but*) that joins two clauses.

My son Ben is a very special child. He is very athletic. He is only two years old, but he can catch a ball. He rides a bicycle, and he never falls. He is also very smart. He writes his name and address, and he knows the alphabet. He is talkative and funny. He talks all the time, but I sometimes don't listen.

Practice 7.3: Combine the two sentences into one sentence. Use the conjunction in parentheses. Don't forget to put a comma *before* the conjunction.

1. (**but**) My niece is smart. She has problems in school. _My niece is_ _smart, but she has problems in school._

2. (**but**) My brother is handsome. He doesn't have a girlfriend. _____ _____

3. (**and**) My mother likes to plant flowers. My father likes to plant vegetables. _____ _____ _____

4. (**but**) Miguel likes jazz. He doesn't like rock. _____ _____

5. (**but**) Juana's job is boring. The pay is good. _____ _____

6. (**and**) The train is expensive. The bus is very slow. _____ _____

7. (**but**) Alice wants to drive to work. She doesn't have a car. _____ _____

8. (**and**) Mario has a job. His wife takes care of their children. _____ _____

Talk about it

Talk to your partner. Complete each sentence.

1. My class is interesting, but _____

2. I like my life, but _____

3. I want a new car, but _____

4. McDonalds is cheap, but _____

Including details in your paragraphs

Details make writing interesting. There are many ways to add details to your paragraphs. For example, after you use an adjective, you can give an example to show why the adjective is true.

Write about it

Work with a partner. Read the paragraphs and answer the questions.

Paragraph 1

My brother Juan is a wonderful person. He is generous. He is hardworking. He is very talented.

Paragraph 2

My brother Juan is a wonderful person. He is generous. He always buys food for our family. He is hardworking. He works six days a week and he takes classes at community college. He is very talented. He plays the guitar and sings. He sometimes plays the guitar at weddings and other celebrations.

1. Which paragraph is more interesting, Paragraph 1 or Paragraph 2? Why? _____

_____

2. What is the proof that Juan is generous? _____

_____

3. What is the proof that Juan is hardworking? _____

_____

4. What is the proof that Juan is talented? _____

_____

Think about it

Work with a partner. Write the number of the sentence in Column B that proves the adjective in column A.

Column A	Column B
1. ___D___ My wife is friendly.	A. He doesn't have a job, and he doesn't clean the house.
2. _____ My son is helpful.	B. She plays all day. She never wants to sleep.
3. _____ My husband is generous.	C. She usually studies for eight hours every day.
4. _____ Peter is lazy.	D. She likes to talk to people, and she has many friends.
5. _____ My baby is active.	E. She has two jobs, and she takes classes at the community college.
6. _____ My daughter is studious.	F. He cleans the house, does the dishes, and washes all the clothes.
7. _____ Griselda is hardworking.	G. He gives me nice gifts on my birthday, Christmas, and Valentine's Day.
8. _____ Edgar is handsome.	H. He is tall and muscular.

Practice 7.4: Write sentences about friends, relatives, or classmates.

- In the first sentence include an adjective that describes the person.

- In the second sentence give an example that proves the adjective is true.

Here is an example.

Sentence with adjective: _My husband is very athletic._

Proof: _He plays soccer, volleyball, and basketball._

1a. Sentence with adjective: _____

1b. Proof: _____

2a. Sentence with adjective: _____

2b. Proof: _____

3a. Sentence with adjective: _____

3b. Proof: _____

Editing challenge

Now you're ready to practice what you've learned.

- Correct the errors in this paragraph. Each error is underlined.
- Rewrite the paragraph.
- Answer the questions. Use a complete sentence.

My sister Irene is a <u>person good</u>. She is athletic. On weekends <u>She</u> <u>run</u> in the park_ and during the week she <u>go</u> to the gym. <u>she</u> is also compassionate. She <u>have</u> a <u>heart big</u>. <u>Often</u> she <u>make</u> food for <u>people homeless.</u> <u>Irene she</u> is hardworking<u>, she</u> is a waitress at a <u>restaurant Mexican</u>. The customers ___ impatient, but Irene is patient. She <u>no</u> angry.

`My sister Irene is` _____

_____

_____

_____

_____

_____

_____

1. Irene is athletic. How do you know? _____

_____

2. Irene is hardworking. How do you know? _____

_____

3. Write four adjectives that describe Irene. _____

_____

4. There are two compound sentences in this paragraph. Write those sentences.

a. _____

_____

b. _____

_____

Preparing to write

You are going to write about a special person. It can be a friend, relative, classmate, or celebrity. Before you start, do the following:

1. Who are you going to write about? _____

2. Complete the table. Write three adjectives that describe the person. Write a sentence that proves that the adjective is true.

Adjective	Proof
a.	
b.	
c.	

3. Write three more adjectives to describe your special person. _____,

   _____, _____

Writing Assignment 7: *A Special Person*

Write a paragraph about a special person.

1. In the top right corner of your paper write the *heading*. The heading includes:

   Your first and last name

   Today's date

   Assignment 7

2. Indent and write a topic sentence.

3. Skip lines.

4. Write between 6 and 9 sentences. Use the chart above to help you.

5. Use at least <u>5 adjectives</u>. Give examples to prove at least 3 of these adjectives.

6. Write at least 1 compound sentence.

7. Use the editing checklist on the next page to check your work. Circle **Yes** or **No** for each item in the checklist.

Writing Assignment 7: Editing Checklist

Editing Checklist		
Format		
1. I have a correct heading.	Yes	No
2. The first line is indented.	Yes	No
3. I skipped lines.	Yes	No
Content		
1. The paragraph has a topic sentence.	Yes	Yes
2. My paragraph has between 6 and 9 sentences.	Yes	No
3. I used at least 5 adjectives. I have proof for 3 adjectives.	Yes	No
4. The paragraph has 1 compound sentence.	Yes	No
Capitalization and punctuation		
1. I used capital letters correctly.	Yes	No
2. I ended each sentence with a period.	Yes	No
Grammar		
1. All sentences have a subject and a verb.	Yes	No
2. I used adjectives correctly.	Yes	No
3. There are no run-on sentences.	Yes	No

Chapter 8

My Hometown

In this chapter you'll write about your hometown.

Luis Martinez
Feb. 14, 2013
Assignment 8

My hometown is Cuzco, Peru. It is an ancient city. There are many Inca ruins. Cuzco has narrow streets and old churches. It is very hilly. My house is on a hill. From my house I can see beautiful vistas. It is very rainy from December to March. Other times it is dry and warm.

Answer each question with a complete sentence.

1. Where is Luis from? _____

_____

2. What is the weather in Cuzco in January? _____

_____

3. Is Cuzco a new city or an old city? _____

_____

4. Does Luis live in a flat part of the city or a hilly part of the city?_____

_____

Adjectives that describe places

In the last chapter you used adjectives to describe people. The following are adjectives that describe cities, towns, and neighborhoods.

_____ small/tiny	_____ quiet/peaceful/calm	_____ interesting
_____ big/large/huge	_____ mountainous/hilly	_____ boring
_____ beautiful/gorgeous	_____ flat	_____ exciting
_____ ugly	_____ clean	_____ rural
_____ busy	_____ dirty	_____ urban
_____ crowded	_____ fun	_____ safe
_____ noisy	_____ romantic	_____ dangerous

These adjectives describe the weather.

_____ hot	_____ cool	_____ rainy
_____ cold	_____ sunny	_____ snowy
_____ warm	_____ cloudy	_____ mild

Talk about it

- Read the adjectives in the boxes above.
- Put a check next to each adjective you know.
- Learn the meanings of adjectives you don't know. Ask your classmates or find the definition in a dictionary.

Write about it

Write 3 adjectives you just learned. Use each adjective in a sentence.

Adjective	Sentence that uses the adjective
1.	
2.	
3.	

Adjectives that describe where you live

Adjectives can also describe a house or apartment. Here are some examples.

_____ small/tiny	_____ organized	_____ old
_____ big/large/huge	_____ disorganized	_____ new
_____ neat	_____ clean	_____ modern
_____ messy	_____ dirty	_____ run-down
_____ bright	_____ comfortable	_____ crowded
_____ dark	_____ cozy	

Talk about it

- Read the adjectives in the box on the prevoius page. Put a check next to each adjective you know.

- Learn the meanings of adjectives you don't know. Ask your classmates or find the definition in a dictionary.

Write about it

Write 3 adjectives you just learned. Use each adjective in a sentence.

Adjective	Sentence that uses the adjective
1.	
2.	
3.	

Talk about it

Read each statement below to your partner. Your partner responds with one sentence. For example,

> My apartment is small, clean, and crowded.

Do not say

> ~~My apartment is small. My apartment is clean. My apartment is crowded.~~

1. Describe your house or apartment. Use at least 3 adjectives.
2. Describe the room where you sleep. Use at least 3 adjectives.
3. Describe your hometown. Use at least 3 adjectives.
4. Describe the city or town where you live now. Use at least 3 adjectives.
5. Describe the weather today. Use at least 3 adjectives.

Making adjectives strong and weak

Read these sentences:

> Lisa is <u>very</u> tired.

> Lucas is <u>a little</u> tired.

Very and *a little* are *adverbs*. Adverbs can describe adjectives.

Think about it

Work with a partner. Read the 2 sentences above. Answer these questions.

1. Do the 2 sentences mean the same thing? _____

2. What adjective is in both sentences? _____

3. Do the adverbs, *very* and *a little*, go before or after the adjective? _____

4. Who is more tired, Lisa or Lucas? _____

These drawings illustrate several adverbs.

The dog is <u>extremely</u> large.	The dog is <u>very</u> large. The dog is <u>really</u> large.	The dog is <u>somewhat</u> large. The dog is <u>quite</u> large. The dog is <u>kind of</u> large.	The dog is <u>a little</u> large.

Practice 8.1: Put the words in order to make a sentence.

1. (very, is, small, our classroom)_____ Our classroom is very small. _____

2. (quite, Juana, beautiful, is)_____

3. (hard, Ning, works, really)_____

4. (have, You, nice, parents, extremely) _____

5. (likes, Marvin, really, clothes, expensive) _____

6. (My house, messy, a little, is)_____

Talk about it

Talk to your partner. In each sentence, use at least one adverb: *extremely*, *very*, *really*, *somewhat*, *kind of*, *quite*, and *a little*. (For example, *I am extremely shy. I am a little heavy. I am somewhat hardworking*.)

1. Describe yourself.
2. Describe your neighborhood.
3. Describe your best friend.
4. Describe your husband, wife, girlfriend, or boyfriend.
5. Describe your classroom.
6. Describe your hometown.

Using *there is* and *there are*

Use *there is* and *there are* to tell where things are located. Use *there is* to talk about one thing.

> <u>There is</u> an elephant in the shower.

Use *there are* to talk about more than one thing.

> <u>There are</u> elephants in the shower.

The contraction for *there is* is *there's.* For example,

> <u>There's</u> a monkey on my refrigerator.

There is no contraction for *there are*. This sentence is not correct.

> ~~There're~~ monkeys on my refrigerator.

In sentences with more than one noun, look at the first noun. If the first noun is singular, use *there is.*

> <u>There is</u> a swing, two new slides, and a soccer field at the park.

If the first noun is plural, use *there are.*

> <u>There are</u> two new slides, a swing, and a soccer field at the park.

Write about it

Work with a partner. Write 4 sentences about your classroom. Start your sentences with *There is*, *There's*, or *There are*. Include at least one adjective in each sentence.

1. _____
   _____
2. _____
   _____
3. _____
   _____
4. _____

Using *there is* and *there are* in negative sentences

To make a negative sentence with *there is*, you can say

> There <u>is not</u> a pizza in the oven.
> There <u>isn't</u> a pizza in the oven.
> There <u>is no</u> pizza in the oven.

To make a negative sentence with *there are*, you can say

> There <u>are not</u> pizzas in the oven.
> There <u>aren't</u> pizzas in the oven.
> There <u>are no</u> pizzas in the oven.

Practice 8.2: Read the following paragraph. Complete the sentences with *is* or *are*. Then answer the questions.

Jack Martinez goes to the University of Colorado. He lives in a dorm. He has a roommate. His room is very small. There _____ two beds, two desks, and two chairs. There _____ also two dressers. There _____ no couch because there isn't space. There _____ a mirror above the sink. There _____ no shower. There _____ a kitchen near his room. He goes to the kitchen to make popcorn or cook a hamburger. There _____ forks and knives in the kitchen. But unfortunately there _____ no plates.

1. Is there a shower in Jack's dorm room? _____

_____

2. Are there plates in Jack's kitchen? _____

_____

3. What furniture is there in Jack's dorm room? _____

_____

Using *have* and *has*

Use *has* when the subject is one person, place, animal, or thing.

Amanda <u>has</u> four children.
My kitchen <u>has</u> a new microwave.
That park <u>has</u> many beautiful trees. It also <u>has</u> lovely gardens.

Use *have* all other times.

I <u>have</u> six brothers.
We <u>have</u> a lot of homework.
The classrooms <u>have</u> many chairs.

Practice 8.3: Read the following paragraph. Complete the sentences with *have* or *has*. Then answer the questions on the next page.

My neighborhood _____ many apartment buildings. It also _____ many other buildings including schools, churches, and two libraries. The libraries _____ books, CDs, and computers. My neighborhood also _____ two parks. Ramos Park _____ playgrounds for children and Lincoln Park _____ soccer fields for adults.

1. How many parks are there in this neighborhood? _____

_____

2. What can you find at the library? _____

_____

3. Write the compound sentence that's in the paragraph. _____

_____

Adding variety to your paragraphs

Paragraphs are more interesting when the sentences have different structures.

Think about it

Work with a partner. Read these paragraphs and answer the questions.

Paragraph 1

My classroom is quite large. It has forty desks. It has twenty computers. It also has a desk for the teacher. It has a bookcase with books for the students. It has four white boards. It has large windows. It is very bright and somewhat clean.

Paragraph 2

My classroom is quite large. There are forty desks. There are twenty computers. There is also a desk for the teacher. There is a bookcase with books for the students. There are four white boards. There are large windows. It is very bright and somewhat clean.

Paragraph 3

My classroom is quite large. It has forty desks. There are twenty computers. It also has a desk for the teacher. It has a bookcase with books for the students. There are four white boards. There are large windows. It is very bright and somewhat clean.

1. In the first paragraph, how many sentences start with *There is* or *There are*? _____

2. In the first paragraph, how many sentences include *has* or *have*? _____

3. In the second paragraph, how many sentences start with *There is* or *There are*? _____

4. In the second paragraph, how many sentences include *has* or *have*? _____

5. In the third paragraph, how many sentences start with *There is* or *There are*? _____

6. In the third paragraph, how many sentences include *has* or *have*? _____

7. Which paragraph has more variety? _____

Talk about it

Work with a partner. Look at the picture. Point to each of these words.

slide	bench	volleyball court
fountain	ducks	volleyball net
swing	pond	monkey bars
trees	flowers	path

Practice 8.4: Look at the picture and follow the instructions. Use the words in the box above or other words.

Write 3 sentences about the picture that start with *There is* or *There are*.

1. _____

2. _____

3. _____

Write 3 sentences about the picture that include *have* or *has*.

1. _____

2. _____

3. _____

Graphic organizers

Graphic organizers make writing easier. Here is a graphic organizer about a student's hometown, Guanajuato, Mexico.

- The middle circle has the name of the student's hometown.

- The first item in each circle is a category (for example, *weather, land, jobs*).

- The other information in the circle describes Guanajuato.

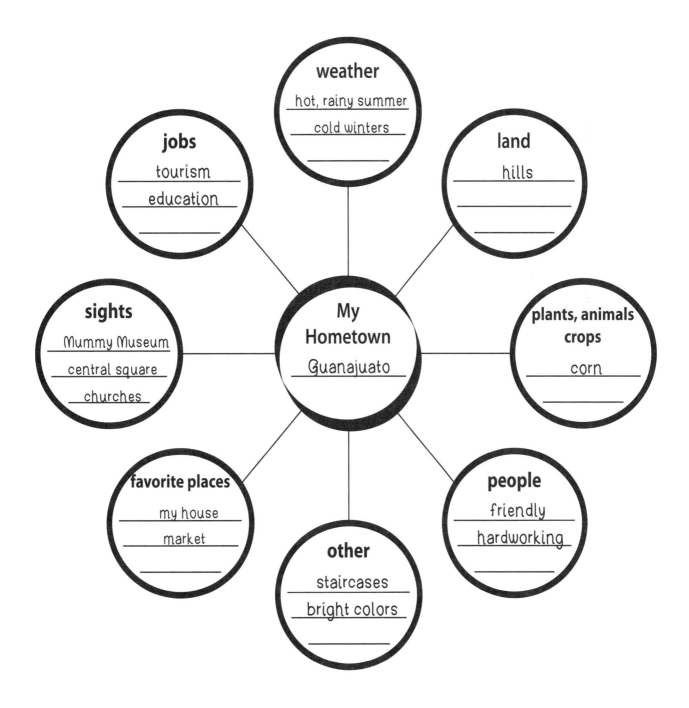

Think about it

Look at the graphic organizer on the previous page. Answer the questions. You don't need to write complete sentences.

1. What is the weather in Guanajuato? _____

_____

2. What are the sights in Guanajuato? _____

_____

3. What kind of jobs are there in Guanajuato? _____

_____

4. What are the author's favorite places in Guanajuato? _____

_____

Editing challenge

Now you're ready to practice what you've learned.

- Correct the errors in this paragraph. Each error is underlined.
- Rewrite the paragraph on the next page.
- Answer the questions about the paragraph.

My hometown is guanajuato Mexico. Is an extremely old city. It have many hills. There are many churches beautiful. In Guanajuato. the building are bright colors, and the people they are extremely friendly and hardworking. Theres the Mummy Museum in Guanajuato it is very famous. In summer Guanajuato is hot and rainy, in winter is a little cold. Guanajuato has a market huge. People sell fruits vetegables and clothes. Many tourists visits Guanajuato.

My hometown is Guanajuato, Mexico.

1. What is the topic sentence of this paragraph? _____

_____

2. What is one detail about the market? _____

_____

3. Who visits Guanajuato? _____

_____

4. What are six adjectives in this paragraph? _____

_____

5. Write one sentence in the paragraph that starts with **There is** or **There are**. _____

_____

6. Write one sentence in the paragraph that includes **have** or **has**._____

_____

7. What is the compound sentence in this paragraph? _____

_____

Preparing to write

You are going to write about your hometown. Use the graphic organizer below.

- Write the name of your hometown in the middle circle.

- Write information about your hometown in at least five of the other circles.

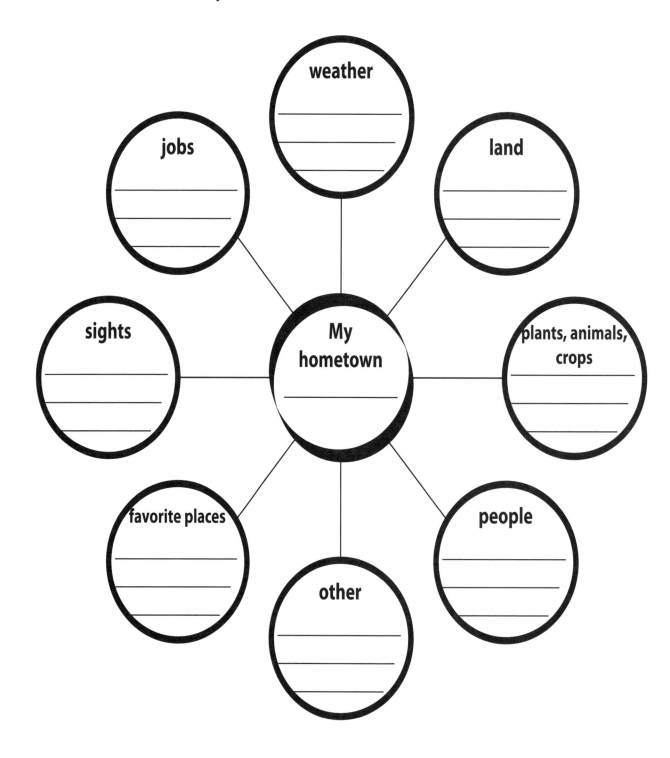

Write about it

- Write between 7 and 10 sentences about your hometown. Use the chart on the previous page to help you.

- Use at least <u>6 adjectives</u>.

- Use *there is* or *there are* in at least 2 sentences.

- Use *have* or *has* in at least 1 sentence.

- Use at least 2 adverbs: *extremely*, *very*, *really*, *somewhat*, *kind of*, *quite*, *a little*.

1. _____

2. _____

3. _____

4. _____

5. _____

6. _____

7. _____

8. _____

9. _____

10. _____

Writing Assignment 8: *My Hometown*

Write a paragraph about your hometown.

1. In the top right corner of your paper write the *heading*. The heading includes:

   Your first and last name

   Today's date

   Assignment 8

2. Indent and write a topic sentence.

3. Skip lines.

4. Write between 7 and 10 more sentences. Copy the sentences in the list above.

5. Use the editing checklist to check your work. Circle *Yes* or *No* for each item in the checklist.

Writing Assignment 8: Editing Checklist

Editing Checklist		
Format		
1. I have a correct heading.	Yes	No
2. The first line is indented.	Yes	No
3. I skipped lines.	Yes	No
Content		
1. The paragraph has a topic sentence.	Yes	Yes
2. My paragraph has between 7 and 10 sentences.	Yes	No
3. I used at least 6 adjectives.	Yes	No
4. I used *there is* or *there are* in at least 2 sentences.	Yes	No
5. I used *have* or *has* in at least 1 sentence.	Yes	No
6. I used 2 adverbs: *extremely*, *very*, *really*, *somewhat*, *kind of*, *quite*, *a little*.	Yes	No
Capitalization and punctuation		
1. I used capital letters correctly.	Yes	No
2. I ended each sentence with a period.	Yes	No
Grammar		
1. All sentences have a subject and a verb.	Yes	No
2. There are no run-on sentences.	Yes	No

Chapter 9

My Hometown: Pros and Cons

In this chapter you'll compare your hometown with where you live now.

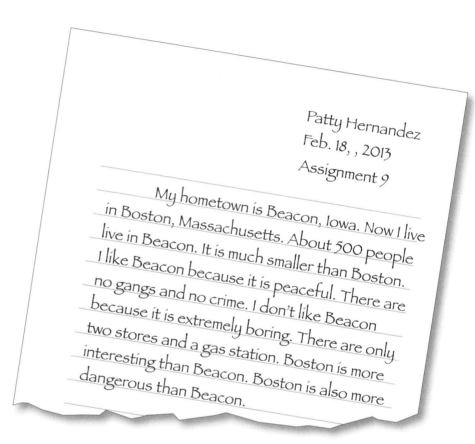

Patty Hernandez
Feb. 18, , 2013
Assignment 9

My hometown is Beacon, Iowa. Now I live in Boston, Massachusetts. About 500 people live in Beacon. It is much smaller than Boston. I like Beacon because it is peaceful. There are no gangs and no crime. I don't like Beacon because it is extremely boring. There are only two stores and a gas station. Boston is more interesting than Beacon. Boston is also more dangerous than Beacon.

Answer each question with a complete sentence.

1. Where does Patty live now? _____

_____

2. Why does Patty like Beacon? _____

_____

3. Is Beacon an exciting town? _____

_____

4. Which is bigger, Beacon or Boston? _____

_____

Simple present vs. present continuous verbs

Earlier in this book you learned about two kinds of present tense verbs: *simple present* and *present continuous*. Here is a summary of when you use these verb tenses.

Verb tense	When to use	Examples
Simple present	To talk about things you do regularly	I <u>study</u> English twice a week.
	To present facts	Alex <u>has</u> two sons.
Present continuous	To talk about things happening right now	Sam <u>is washing</u> his car.

Practice 9.1: Put 2 lines under the correct verb and one line under the subject. Then write *SP* if the verb is *simple present* or *PC* if the verb is *present continuous*.

1. <u>We</u> (<u>work</u>, are working) six days a week.	SP
2. My husband and I usually (watch, are watching) TV at night.	
3. My kids (watch, are watching) TV right now.	
4. Please be quiet. The students (take, are taking) a test.	
5. Your daughter (cries, is crying) now, and I don't know why.	
6. My son (vacuums, is vacuuming) the rug and (cleans, is cleaning) the bathroom every Saturday.	
7. Before a party, we always (put on, are putting on) makeup and (fix, are fixing) our hair.	
8. It (rains, is raining) now, and I don't have an umbrella.	
9. The movie is not funny, but everyone (laughs, is laughing).	
10. Everyone is busy. My sister (does, is doing) her homework. My brother (plays, is playing) video games, and I (read, am reading).	
11. We usually (go, are going) to bed at 10:00 during the week and at 11:00 on weekends.	
12. Right now, I (work, am working), and my husband (takes care, is taking care) of the children.	
13. Luis never (forgets, is forgetting) his homework.	
14. I usually (study, am studying) in the library, but today I (study, am studying) at home.	

Think about it

Ana is visiting her family in El Salvador. She wrote this email to her boyfriend Mario. Complete her email using the verbs in the box. Use simple present or present continuous verbs.

listen	cook	walk	clean
wake up	repeat	watch	relax

From: AnaOrtizzz@yahoo.com

Subject: I miss you!

Date: 12/17/2012

To: MarioHottie@Gmail.com

Hey Mario,

Right now I am at my house in El Salvador. I _____ TV. My mother is in the kitchen. She _____ dinner. My father _____ on the porch. Every day here is the same. I _____ at 7:00.

Then, after breakfast, my mother and I _____ our house. We _____ to music and, in the afternoon, we _____ to the market to buy food. We repeat the same routine every day. It's a little boring. I miss you!

Talk about it

Ask your partner these questions about Ana's email.

- Where is Ana?
- What is she doing now?
- What is her father doing?
- What is her mother doing?
- What time does she get up?
- What does she do in the afternoon?

Action verbs and non-action verbs

Most verbs are *action* verbs. They describe an action. Examples of action verbs are **walk**, **play**, and **write**. Other verbs are *non-action* verbs or *stative* verbs. These verbs do not describe an action. Here are some non-action verbs.

_____ believe	_____ know	_____ need	_____ see	_____ understand
_____ hate	_____ like	_____ prefer	_____ smell	_____ want
_____ hear	_____ love	_____ remember	_____ taste	

Talk about it

- Read the verbs in the box on the previous page. Put a check next to each verb you know.
- If you don't understand a verb, ask a classmate or find the definition in a dictionary.

Using non-action verbs correctly

Use non-action verbs in the simple present tense. For example,

> I <u>know</u> the answer.
>
> I <u>prefer</u> Chinese food.

You usually do not use non-action verbs in the present continuous tense. These sentences are not correct.

> I ~~am knowing~~ the answer.
>
> I ~~am preferring~~ Chinese food.

Write about it

Look at the list of non-action verbs on the previous page. Write three verbs you just learned. Use each verb in a sentence. Use the simple present tense.

Non-action verb	Sentence that uses this verb
1.	
2.	
3.	

Using *like*, *need*, and *want* followed by a noun

In this section you'll learn to use three important non-action verbs: *like*, *need*, and *want*. Study these sentences.

> I like fast <u>cars</u>.
>
> My daughter needs a <u>job</u> as soon as possible.
>
> Frankie wants a new <u>computer</u>.

Think about it

What are the underlined words in the three sentences above?

> a. adjectives
>
> b. nouns
>
> c. verbs

Write about it

1. Write a sentence about what kind of pizza you like. Use *like* followed by a noun. _____

_____

2. Write a sentence about what you need at the grocery store. Use *need* followed by a noun.

_____

3. Write a sentence about what you want to want to buy at the mall. Use *want* followed by a

noun. _____

Using *like, need,* and *want* followed by an infinitive

You can also follow *like*, *need*, and *want* with an *infinitive*. An infinitive has this form.

> to + base verb

Here are some examples. The infinitive in each sentence is underlined.

> I want <u>to live</u> in a big city.
>
> Ning needs <u>to pay</u> the phone bill.
>
> Francis likes <u>to go</u> to casinos in Las Vegas.

Write about it

1. Write a sentence about what you like to do in your free time. Use *like* followed by an

infinitive. _____

2. Write a sentence about what you need to do tomorrow. Use *need* followed by an infinitive.

_____

3. Write a sentence about what you want to study. Use *want* followed by an infinitive. _____

_____

Think about it

- Read each sentence.
- Put 2 lines under the non-action verb.
- Put 1 line under the subject.
- Write *N* if the bold type is a noun. Write *I* if the bold type is an infinitive.

	Noun (N) or Infinitive (I)?
1. I need **to buy** a car.	I
2. Joseph wants a **girlfriend**.	
3. You need **to work** late today.	
4. Frita and Diego like **to paint** beautiful pictures.	
5. Alexander doesn't like **tamales**.	

	Noun (N) or Infinitive (I)?
6. We want **to move** to Texas.	
7. My brother likes **tennis** and **soccer**.	
8. On Monday, Liliana needs **to take** her car to the mechanic.	

Practice 9.2

- Read the sentences in the chart.

- If the sentence is correct, put an X in the *Correct* box.

- If the sentence is incorrect, put an X in the *Incorrect* box and correct the error. Some sentences have more than one correct answer.

	Correct	Incorrect
to 1. I need study English to get a better job.		X
2. I like to pizza.		
3. My kids like to eat pizza.		
4. Anastasia likes draw pictures of people.		
5. Lionel needs to work overtime next week.		
6. My parents need to a microwave.		
7. They need a job.		
8. We want go to college.		
9. Arnoldo likes to Mexico.		
10. The children like to play in the water.		

Talk about it

1. Tell your partner 2 places you want to visit. Start your sentence with *I want to visit…*

2. Tell your partner three fruits you like. Start you sentence with *I like…*

3. Tell your partner five things you need at the grocery story. Start your sentence, *At the grocery store I need…*

4. Tell your partner 2 subjects you want to study (for example, *English, math, history, French, Spanish, Chinese, biology,* etc.). Start your sentence with *I want to study…*

Write about it

1. What subjects does your partner want to study? _____

   _____

2. What places does your partner want to visit? _____

   _____

3. What fruits does your partner like? _____

   _____

4. What does your partner need at the grocery store? _____

   _____

Comparative adjectives

An adjective describes a noun or pronoun. *Big*, *small*, *happy*, and *sad* are adjectives. *Comparative adjectives* compare nouns and pronouns. *Bigger*, *smaller*, *happier*, and *sadder* are comparative adjectives.

Talk about it
- Look at the pictures.
- Underline the comparative adjective.
- Write *T* if the statement is *True* and *F* if the statement is *False*.

Barney	Lassie	Rover	Pooch

	T or F
1. Pooch is <u>shorter</u> than Lassie.	F
2. Pooch is taller than Barney.	
3. Rover is shorter than Barney.	
4. Barney is taller than Pooch.	
5. Lassie is darker than Pooch.	
6. Pooch is darker than Rover.	

Forming comparative adjectives

If an adjective

- has one syllable

or

- has *more than one syllable* and ends in **y**

use this form to create the comparative adjective.

Adjective	Comparative adjective (adjective + **er** + **than***)
big	big<u>ger</u> than
funny	funn<u>ier</u> than

For example,

New York is <u>bigger than</u> Seattle.

My teacher is <u>funnier than</u> your teacher.

If the adjective has 2 or more syllables and *does not* end in **y**, use this form.

Adjective	Comparative adjective (**more** + adjective + **than**)
expensive	<u>more</u> expensive than
interesting	<u>more</u> interesting than

For example,

That green sweater is <u>more expensive than</u> the blue sweater.

My ESL class is <u>more interesting than</u> my math class.

These adjectives are irregular in the comparative form.

Adjective	Comparative adjective (Irregular comparative adjective + **than**)
good	<u>better</u> than
bad	<u>worse</u> than
far	<u>farther</u> than

Here are some examples:

Pizza Castle is <u>better than</u> Pop's Pizza.

The weather in New York is <u>worse than</u> the weather in my country.

My tennis court is <u>farther than</u> the park.

*Rules for spelling comparative adjectives are in Appendix A.

Think about it

Write the comparative form of each adjective.

1. tired ___more tired than___	11. clean _____
2. thin _____	12. pretty _____
3. interesting _____	13. silly _____
4. heavy _____	14. nice _____
5. crazy _____	15. happy _____
6. late _____	16. famous _____
7. nervous _____	17. bad _____
8. good _____	18. boring _____
9. beautiful _____	19. cold _____
10. dark_____	20. far _____

Common mistakes with comparative adjectives

Don't say *more better*.

Incorrect	Correct
I feel ~~more better~~ than yesterday.	I feel <u>better</u> than yesterday.

Don't use *more* with one syllable adjectives or adjectives that end in *y*.

Incorrect	Correct
Florida is ~~more hot~~ than Oregon.	Florida is <u>hotter</u> than Oregon.
Alice is ~~more crazy~~ than her sister.	Alice is <u>crazier</u> than her sister.

Practice 9.3

- Read the sentences in the chart.
- If the sentence is correct, put an X in the *Correct* box.
- If the sentence is incorrect, put an X in the *Incorrect* box and correct the error.

	Correct	Incorrect
~~harder~~ 1. This test is ~~more hard~~ than our last test.		X
2. Ana is more beautiful than her sister.		
3. This class is more hard than my last class.		

	Correct	Incorrect
4. The apples are more better than the peaches.		
5. My brother is more thin than me.		
6. I am heavier than Carlos.		
7. This pizza is more better than the pizza at Pop's Pizza.		
8. I feel more bad today than yesterday.		
9. My ESL class is bigger than my math class.		
10. I am more busier today than yesterday.		
11. My new boss is nicer than my old boss.		
12. This class is more hard than my last class.		

Talk about it

Talk to your partner. Compare each pair of nouns. Use comparative adjectives. For example, for the first item say, **An ant is smaller than a lion.**

1. a lion an ant (*small*)	4. January July (*cold*)	7. navy blue light blue (*light*)
2. the sun the moon (*far*)	5. Coke water (*healthy*)	8. my hometown this town (*beautiful*)
3. El Salvador United States (*big*)	6. a turtle a cheetah (*fast*)	9. a table a feather (*heavy*)

Talk about it

Compare yourself to your partner. Use comparative adjectives. For example, for the first item say, **Your hair is longer than my hair** or **My hair is longer than your hair.**

1. my hair your hair (*long*)	3. my eyes your eyes (*big*)	5. my hair your hair (*curly*)
2. my arms your arms (*short*)	4. my shoes your shoes (*new*)	6. my notebook your notebook (*neat*)

Write about it

Work with a partner. Write 5 sentences that compare these students. Use the adjectives in parentheses.

ID Card: Vista College	ID Card: Vista College
Name: Ann Lee	Name: Liz Mendez
Phone number: 560-333-1111	Phone number: 560-687-5698
Date of birth: 7/5/91	Date of birth: 5/8/90
Height: 5'8"	Height: 5'6"
Weight: 128 lbs.	Weight: 139 lbs.

1 (heavy) <u>Liz is heavier than Ann.</u> _____

2. (tall) _____

3. (old) _____

4. (young) _____

5. (thin) _____

6. (short) _____

Using *because*

Conjunctions are joining words. You learned that you use the conjunctions **and** and **but** to join 2 clauses. For example,

> I am tired, <u>and</u> I need to take a nap.

> I am tired, <u>but</u> I don't have time to take a nap.

Because is also a conjunction. You use **because** to join a main clause and a *because* clause. Here is the form.

Main clause	*Because* clause
<u>You</u> <u>need</u> an umbrella	(because) <u>it</u> <u>is</u> raining.

Notice the following:

- This sentence has 2 clauses, a *main* clause and a *because* clause.
- Each clause has a subject and a verb.
- A *because* clause is *not* a complete sentence. It is not correct to say

> ~~Because it is raining.~~

You also can start sentences with a *because* clause followed by a main clause. When you start a sentence with a *because* clause, put a comma after the *because* clause. Here is the form.

Because clause	Main clause
(Because) <u>it</u> <u>is</u> raining,	<u>you</u> <u>need</u> an umbrella.

Practice 9.4

- Circle the conjunction *because*.

- Put 2 lines under the verb in each clause. Put 1 line under the subject.

1. The <u>employees</u> <u>are</u> tired (because) they <u>work</u> overtime every day.

2. Elena speaks English fluently because she practices every day.

3. Your car doesn't start because it needs gas.

4. My sister can't come to the party because she has a fever.

5. I need to go to the grocery store because we don't have food for dinner.

6. Because your appointment is in fifteen minutes, we need to hurry.

7. The children need to go to bed early because they have school tomorrow.

8. Because it is very hot today, you need to water your plants.

Think about it

Work with a partner.

- If the sentence is complete, put an X in the *Complete* column.

- If the sentence is incomplete, put an X in the *Incomplete* column.

	Complete	Incomplete
1. Because I need more money.		X
2. I like to relax on weekends.		
3. Angi wants to get a job because she needs to earn money.		
4. Today is a beautiful day.		
5. Because it is a beautiful day, I want to go to the beach.		
6. I want to be outside because today is a beautiful day.		
7. Because he is a wonderful person.		
8. I want to marry my boyfriend.		
9. I want to marry my boyfriend because he is a wonderful person.		
10. Because we need to arrive on time.		
11. I always do my homework.		
12. Because the class is difficult, I always do my homework.		

Think about it

Do the following:

- If the sentence is correct, check the *Correct* box.
- If the sentence is not correct, check the *Incorrect* box. Correct the sentence.

	Correct	Incorrect
she 1. My daughter has a scholarship because is a very good student.		X
2. I like my class because is very interesting.		
3. The students are late because the bus didn't come.		
4. I often give my mother a ride because doesn't have a car.		
5. I need to study because is difficult the class.		
6. You need to go to sleep because is late.		
7. Yvonne is absent because he sick.		
8. You need to wear a jacket because is cold outside.		

Talk about it

Ask your partner the following questions. Use ***because*** in your answer and answer with a complete sentence. For example, the answer to the first question might be ***I prefer to eat at home because restaurants are quite expensive***.

1. Do you prefer to eat dinner at home or to eat out? Why?

2. Do you prefer to live in the country or in the city? Why?

3. What is your favorite season? Why?

4. What is your favorite TV show? Why?

5. Who is your favorite singer? Why?

Write about it

Answer each question with a complete sentence.

1. Why do you want to study English? _____

_____

2. Why do you want to live in the United States? _____

More about details

Comparative adjectives and *because* clauses make writing interesting. Read this paragraph. The author is from Reykjvik, Iceland. Today, she lives in Seattle, Washington.

>   My hometown is Reykjvik, Iceland. Now I live in Seattle, Washington. I like my hometown because it is a friendly place. The people are kind, and I have many friends. The people in Reykjvik are friendlier than the people in Seattle. I also like my hometown because the weather is very cold, and I love cold weather. Reykjvik is much colder than Seattle. I don't like my hometown because food and clothes are extremely expensive. For example, a medium pizza in Reykjvik costs about $20. I also don't like my hometown because winter days are very short. In December we only have four hours of sunlight each day.

Write about it

1. Write 2 sentences in the paragraph that include comparative adjectives.

1a. _____

1b. _____

2. Write one sentence from the paragraph with a *because* clause. _____

_____

3. Write one detail about the prices in Reykjvik. _____

_____

4. Write one detail about the length of the days in Reykjvik. _____

_____

5. Which topics does the author write about in this paragraph? Underline 3 answers.

    a. weather   d. buildings   g. government

    b. prices   e. education   h. opportunities

    c. shopping   f. people   i. scenery

Editing challenge

Now you're ready to practice what you've learned.

- Read the paragraph on the next page. The author is from Bejing, China. Now she lives in Rockford, Illinois.
- Correct the errors. Each error is underlined.
- Rewrite the paragraph.
- Answer the questions on the next page.

My hometown is Bejing, China. Now <u>live</u> in Rockford, Illinois. I like my hometown because there are many <u>buildings historic</u> and beautiful parks. At the park I <u>exercises</u>, relax, and play chess. I also like <u>to</u> my hometown because the <u>food it</u> is <u>wonderful</u>, My <u>foods favorite</u> are kung pao <u>chicken,</u> and Peking duck. The food in Bejing is spicier _____ the food in Rockford. I <u>no like</u> my hometown <u>because is</u> polluted. It is difficult <u>often</u> to breath. <u>Bejing it</u> is more polluted than Rockford. I also don't like Bejing because the <u>laws very</u> strict. The <u>law</u> in Bejing are <u>more stricter</u> than the laws in the U.S.

_____

_____

_____

_____

_____

_____

_____

_____

_____

Answer with a complete sentence.

1. What three comparative adjectives are used in this paragraph? _____

_____

2. Write one sentence in the paragraph that has a *because* clause. _____

_____

3. Describe the food in Bejing. _____

_____

4. Is Bejing more polluted than Rockford? _____

_____

Writing Assignment 9: Preparing to write

For this assignment you will compare your hometown with where you live now.

1. From the list below, choose at least four categories and list them in column 1.

a. weather	g. buildings
b. prices	h. education
c. shopping	i. people
d. laws	j. government
e. scenery	k. opportunities
f. nightlife	l. food

2. In Column 2, write a sentence that compares your hometown and where you live now. (For example, the category is *weather*. You live in Miami and your hometown is Bejing. You could write

The weather in Miami is hotter than the weather in Bejing.

Column 1: Category	Column 2: Comparatison
1.	
2.	
3.	
4.	
5.	
6.	

3. Why do you like your hometown? _____

_____

4. Why do you like where you live now? _____

_____

Writing Assignment 9: *My Hometown: Pros and Cons*

Write a paragraph that compares your hometown to where you live now.

1. In the top right corner of your paper write the heading.

2. Indent and write these two topic sentences.

    My hometown is _____. Now I live in _____ .

4. Write between 7 and 10 sentences. Use the chart on the previous page to help you.

5. Use at least 4 comparative adjectives.

6. Include at least 2 sentences with a *because* clause.

7. Use the editing checklist to check your work. Circle **Yes** or **No** for each item in the checklist.

Writing Assignment 9: Editing Checklist

Editing Checklist		
Format		
1. I have a correct heading.	Yes	No
2. The first line is indented.	Yes	No
3. I skipped lines.	Yes	No
Content		
1. The paragraph has a topic sentence.	Yes	Yes
2. My paragraph has between 7 and 10 sentences.	Yes	No
3. I used at least 4 comparative adjectives.	Yes	No
4. There are 2 sentences with a *because* clause.	Yes	No
Capitalization and punctuation		
1. I used capital letters correctly.	Yes	No
2. I ended each sentence with a period.	Yes	No
Grammar		
1. All sentences have a subject and a verb.	Yes	No
2. There are no run-on sentences.	Yes	No

Chapter 10

What I Did Yesterday

In this chapter you'll write about what you did yesterday.

Luis Martinez

Feb. 14, 2013

Assignment 10

Yesterday was a crazy day. First, my alarm clock didn't go off. Then I missed the bus. I walked to my job at Pizza Plus, but I arrived an hour late. My boss was angry. After that, the oven at the restaurant broke. We couldn't make pizzas. We closed the restaurant for lunch. The customers were upset. After work I went home, ate a sandwich, watched TV, and went to bed. I was happy to end the day.

Answer each question with a complete sentence.

1. How did Luis get to work? _____

_____

2. What broke? _____

_____

3. What did Luis do yesterday evening? _____

_____

4. What are five past tense verbs in this paragraph? _____

_____

The simple past: *to be*

You use the past of *to be* to talk about things that started and ended in the past. Study this table.

Subject	Past of verb *to be*	Rest of the sentence
I /He/She/It	was	ready at 2:00.
You/We/They	were	ready at 2:00.

Think about it

Work with a partner. Complete each sentence with *was* or *were*.

1. My sister __was__ sick on Monday.

2. We _____ at work yesterday.

3. It _____ kind of hot on Wednesday.

4. Last year Juana and Janice _____ in Honduras.

5. My parents and I _____ at home on Saturday.

6. The students _____ in the library all day yesterday.

7. Yesterday I _____ worried because my daughter _____ very sick.

8. My car _____ at the body shop yesterday.

9. My daughter and I _____ really tired yesterday.

10. Louisa _____ in Los Angeles yesterday, and Tony _____ in San Francisco.

11. The scientists _____ in their laboratory all day yesterday.

12. My boss and I _____ at work last night.

13. Yesterday my daughter _____ unhappy because her teacher _____ absent.

14. We _____ at the park yesterday morning, but it _____ very cold and windy.

15. Yesterday afternoon I _____ at the mall and Jonathan _____ at a baseball game.

Talk about it

Work with a partner. Partner A reads the sentence in Column 1. Partner B changes the sentence to the past tense. This is a conversation activity. Do not write the answers.

Column 1: Present	Column 2: Past
1. I am tired.	_____ yesterday.
2. I am at work.	_____ yesterday.
3. My boss is angry.	_____ yesterday.
4. Ben and Ana are at the mall.	Yesterday, _____.
5. My mother and I are busy.	Yesterday, _____.
6. My children are sick.	_____ yesterday.
7. My uncle is at a baseball game.	_____ yesterday.
8. Jack is at his cousin's house.	Yesterday, _____.
9. I am available.	Yesterday, _____.
10. We are at home.	Yesterday, _____.

Negative past tense sentences with *to be*

Use *was not* or *were not* in negative sentences with *to be*. To use a contraction, change *was not* to *wasn't* and *were not* to *weren't*. Here is the form.

Subject	Past of verb *to be*	Rest of the sentence
I /He/She/It	was not	ready at 2:00.
	wasn't	ready at 2:00.
You/We/They	were not	ready at 2:00.
	weren't	ready at 2:00.

Talk about it

Tell your partner how you felt yesterday. Use adjectives from the table. Use *was* and *wasn't*. (For example, *I was busy yesterday. I wasn't tired yesterday.*)

active	happy	bored
busy	lazy	relaxed
tired	industrious	worried
exhausted	frustrated	anxious

Practice 10.1

- Change each sentence from present to past.
- Include *yesterday* in all past tense sentences.

Present	Past
1. Ana and Margaret are at home today.	Ana and Margaret were at home yesterday.
2. I am bored.	
3. Andrew is not at school.	
4. My parents are on a trip.	
5. Mario isn't at school.	
6. Louisa and Jerome aren't at the gym.	
7. I'm not sick.	
8. Clara and I are not busy.	
9. The school is not open.	
10. My girlfriend is angry because I am late.	
11. That restaurant isn't open.	
12. Veronica is absent.	
13. It's a sunny day.	
14. I am at home, and my sister is at work.	
15. Fred is happy, because he is with his girlfriend.	

Talking about the past

Here are some expressions you use to talk about the past.

yesterday....	this...	last...
yesterday morning	this morning	last night
yesterday afternoon	this afternoon	last week
yesterday evening	this evening	last month
the day before yesterday		last year

You use the expressions *this morning*, *this afternoon*, *this evening*, and *tonight* to talk about things that happened earlier in the day. For example,

> **This morning** I washed my hair.

Put past time expressions at the beginning of the sentence or at the end of the sentence. If the expression is at the beginning of a sentence, you can put a comma after it. The comma is optional.

> **Yesterday,** I was in Los Angeles.
> **Yesterday** I was in Los Angeles.
> I was in Los Angeles **yesterday.**

Do not put the time expression in the middle of the sentence.

> I ~~yesterday~~ was in Los Angeles.
> I was ~~yesterday~~ in Los Angeles.

It is correct to say,

> I was in Los Angeles **yesterday in the morning**.

It is better to say,

> I was in Los Angeles **yesterday morning**.

Talk about it

- Tell your partner when you were at each of the places in the table below. Tell the truth.

- Use *was* and *wasn't* and time expressions from the previous page (*yesterday morning*, *yesterday afternoon*, etc.).

For example, *I was at home yesterday morning. I wasn't at school last week.*

at home/at my house	at school
at work	at church
at the mall	at the laundromat
at the park	at the grocery store
at the gym	at my friend's house

Talk about it

Repeat the previous exercise for someone else. (For example, *My husband was at the gym yesterday morning. My husband wasn't at the mall last night.*)

Write about it

Write a sentence about where you were yesterday morning, yesterday afternoon, and yesterday evening.

1. _____

2. _____

3. _____

More about past tense verbs

There are 2 kinds of past tense verbs:

- *regular* past tense verbs
- *irregular* past tense verbs

Regular past tense verbs

Regular past tense verbs end in **ed**. To make a regular past tense verb, add **ed** to the base verb. Here is the form.

Subject	Regular past tense verb	Rest of the sentence
I /He/She/It/You/We/They	work<u>ed</u>	last night.

Rules for spelling regular past tense verbs are in Appendix A.

Talk about it

Tell your partner 5 things you did yesterday. Tell the truth.

- Use verbs in the table below. The letters in parentheses tell you how to pronounce the ending sound of the verb.
- Use time expressions (***yesterday morning***, ***yesterday afternoon***, ***last night***, etc.).

For example, ***I worked yesterday morning. I watched TV last night.***

worked (*t*)	visited (*ed*)
studied (*d*)	played (*d*)
watched (*t*)	walked (*t*)
cooked (*t*)	picked up (*t*)
cleaned (*d*)	washed (*t*)
listened (*d*)	exercised (*d*)
called (*d*)	talked (*t*)
helped (*t*)	prepared (*d*)

Practice 10.2: Use verbs from the box to complete the paragraph.

play	bake	call
be	celebrate	talk
relax	grill	

Yesterday was a terrific day. We _____ my nephew's birthday. We had

a big party in the park. I made a huge salad. My brother _____ chicken and

steak on the grill. My sister is an excellent baker. She _____ a chocolate cake.

It _____ delicious. After we ate, some people _____ soccer.

Other people _____ on the grass. Then my nephew _____ his

mother in Guatemala. Everyone _____ to her.

Irregular past tense verbs

Irregular past tense verbs do not end in **ed**. For example, the past tense of **drink** is **drank**. It is not **drinked**. Here is the form.

Subject	Irregular past tense verb	Rest of the sentence
I /He/She/It/You/We/They	drank	champagne at the wedding.

Think about it

Work with a partner. Write **R** for *Regular* or **I** for *Irregular* after each verb. (If a verb ends in **ed**, it is *regular*. If a verb doesn't end in **ed**, it is *irregular*.)

1.	walked	R	10.	saw	_____
2.	studied	_____	11.	took	_____
3.	came	_____	12.	lived	_____
4.	went	_____	13.	ate	_____
5.	worked	_____	14.	watched	_____
6.	drank	_____	15.	cried	_____
7.	was	_____	16.	put	_____
8.	played	_____	17.	sang	_____
9.	did	_____	18.	read	

Think About It

Work with a partner. Write the past tense of each irregular verb. If you don't know the irregular form, look in Appendix B.

1. go _____	9. see _____
2. eat _____	10. say _____
3. drink _____	11. do _____
4. come _____	12. have _____
5. forget _____	13. begin _____
6. take _____	14. put _____
7. think _____	15. pay _____
8. buy _____	16. meet _____

Practice 10.3: Write the past tense form of the verb. If you don't know if a verb is irregular, see Appendix B.

1. (work) I _____ late yesterday.

2. (go) Andrew _____ to visit his sister this morning.

3. (cry) My daughter _____ yesterday because she was sick.

4. (study) We _____ for three hours last night.

5. (start) I _____ my new job in January.

6. (buy) My wife_____ new shoes last week.

7. (have) My girlfriend and I _____ a great time at the party.

8. (spend) We _____ a lot of money at the mall on Saturday.

9. (visit, drink, eat) My best friend _____ me yesterday, and we _____ coffee and _____ cake.

10. (play) The boys _____ soccer for two hours yesterday.

11. (forget, leave) I _____ my keys at my house, and I _____ my wallet on the bus.

12. (watch) We _____ a scary movie last night.

13. (be, work) I _____ at home last night, but my husband _____.

14. (play, sing) At the party, I _____ the piano, and everyone _____.

More practice with time expressions

You have used time expressions with *was* and *were*. Now you'll use time expressions with all other past tense verbs.

Put past time expressions at the beginning of the sentence or at the end of the sentence. If the expression is at the beginning of a sentence, the comma is optional.

   Yesterday, I worked late.   **Yesterday** I worked late.   I worked late **yesterday**.

Do not put the time expression in the middle of the sentence.

   I ~~yesterday~~ worked late.   I worked ~~yesterday~~ late.

Practice 10.4: Put the words in order. Use the words in parentheses.

   • In the first sentence, put the time expression at the beginning of the sentence.

   • In the second sentence, put the time expression at the end of the sentence.

Remember: Don't put time expressions in the middle of a sentence!

1. (yesterday, worked, late, Ramon)

1a. ___Ramon worked late yesterday._____

1b. ___Yesterday, Ramon worked late._____

2. (called, my brother, last week, I)

2a. _____

2b. _____

3. (did, last week, my homework, I)

3a. _____

3b. _____

4. (Fred and Louisa, last February, got married)

4a. _____

4b. _____

5. (to Seattle, my parents, yesterday morning, went)

5a. _____

5b. _____

6. (last week, took, an exam, the students)

6a. _____

6b. _____

7. (was, last night, Nabil, in the hospital)

7a. _____

7b. _____

Negative sentences with past tense verbs

You use **was not** and **were not** for negative past tense sentences with **to be**. To make a sentence in the past negative that doesn't have **to be**, place **did not** or **didn't** before the *base form* of the verb.

Subject	*did*	base form of verb	Rest of the sentence
I/He/She/It/We/You/They	did not didn't	work	yesterday.

Study these examples.

Simple past affirmative	Simple past negative: *did not*	Simple past negative: *didn't*
I <u>worked</u> on Saturday.	I <u>did not work</u> on Sunday.	I <u>didn't work</u> on Sunday.
Lisa <u>found</u> her keys.	Lisa <u>did not find</u> her wallet.	Lisa <u>didn't find</u> her wallet.
Lin <u>went</u> to the mall.	Lin <u>did not go</u> to the park.	Lin <u>didn't go</u> to the park.

Practice 10.5

- Put 2 lines under the past tense verb in Column 1.
- Write the negative sentence in Column 2.

Column 1: Affirmative sentences	Column 2: Negative sentences
1. Alex <u>visited</u> his parents yesterday.	Alex didn't visit his parents yesterday.
2. Laura played tennis last night.	
3. My boyfriend called me yesterday.	
4. My parents went to Florida.	
5. Ana and Roberto had a baby last week.	
6. The baby cried a lot.	
7. I saw your sister yesterday.	
8. My co-workers worked overtime.	
9. I locked the door this morning.	

Talk about it

Tell your partner 6 things you did yesterday and 6 things you didn't do. Use the verbs in the box or use other verbs. (For example, *I worked yesterday. I didn't exercise.*)

work	exercise	make breakfast	go to the park
do the laundry	clean	eat breakfast	go to church
do homework	listen to music	drink coffee	go shopping
do the dishes	call	visit	pick up

Think about it

- Read the story.
- Correct the sentences below. Write 1 true negative sentence and 1 true affirmative sentence.

  Yesterday was an unusual day for Soledad. It was a Saturday. She woke up at 9:00. The house was empty. Soledad's children were on a special school trip. Her husband was at work. She liked her quiet house. She made a cup of coffee and listened to music. After that, she washed some clothes and sewed a pair of pants. She watched soccer on TV. Because she was hungry, she made a sandwich for lunch. After lunch, she ran in the park. When she came home, she called her mother. She looked at her watch. It was 5:30. She was lonely. She missed her family.

Incorrect sentence	Correct sentences
1. Soledad woke up at 7:00.	`Soledad didn't wake up at 7:00. She woke up at 9:00.`
2. Soledad drank tea.	
3. Soledad walked in the park.	
4. Soledad washed the dishes.	
5. She sewed her dress.	
6. Soledad's husband was at home.	
7. She ate a sandwich for dinner.	
8. She watched the news on TV.	
9. She felt happy in the evening.	

Time order words

Use *time order words* to talk about events in the past. Here are some time order words you learned before.

first   next   then   after that   later   finally

Time order words go at the *beginning* of the sentence. You can put a comma after the time order word. It is optional.

First I went to work. After that I went to my class.

First, I went to work. After that, I went to my class.

Talk about it

Work with a partner. Number the sentences from 1 to 7. Number 1 is the first thing that Michael did and Number 7 is the last thing that he did.

_____Then he took a bowl from the cabinet.

_____ Finally, he put the eggs on his plate and had a delicious breakfast.

_____ He cracked three eggs into the bowl and mixed them.

_____ After that, he poured the eggs into a pan.

_____ First, he took the eggs out of the refrigerator.

_____ He stirred the eggs until they were cooked.

___1___ Michael made scrambled eggs for breakfast.

Write about it

Write a paragraph about how you recently prepared a simple food. Use <u>at least</u> 4 time order words (***first***, ***next***, ***then***, ***after that***, ***later***, ***finally***). Use past tense verbs in the box below or other verbs.

mixed *(t)*	stirred *(d)*	put
poured *(d)*	cooked *(t)*	boiled *(d)*
baked *(t)*	added *(ed)*	fried *(d)*

_____

_____

_____

_____

_____

Talk about it

Read your paragraph to your partner.

Talk about it

Tell your partner 6 things you did yesterday. Use time order words (*first*, *next*, *then*, *after that*, *later*, *finally*).

Write about it

Write a paragraph about what your partner did yesterday. Write at least 4 sentences. Use time order words (*first*, *next*, *then*, *after that*, *later*, *finally*).

_____

_____

_____

_____

_____

Approximate time expressions

Sometimes you don't know exactly when something happened. In those cases, use **around** or **about**. The following sentences have the same meaning.

> I ate dinner at <u>about</u> 7:00.

> I went to bed at <u>around</u> 11:00.

Talk about it

Ask your partner the following questions:

- What did you do at about 9:00 this morning?
- What did you do at around 2:00 yesterday afternoon?
- Where were you at about 8:00 last night?
- Where were you at around noon yesterday?
- Where were you at around 11:00 yesterday morning?

Editing challenge

Now you're ready to practice what you've learned.

- Read the paragraph.
- Correct the errors. Each error is underlined.
- Rewrite the paragraph.
- Answer the questions on the next page.

Yesterday was a day busy. I woke at 7:00. Then, I waked up my baby. I gave my baby breakfast, after that I took my baby to the Babysitter and drove to work. I arrive at work 8:00. Next I drove my bus for three hour. My break was only 15 minute. I no have time for lunch. I drive my bus for four more hours, then I pick up my baby from the babysitter. I make dinner. but I no have time to eat. After that I taked my baby back to the babysitter. Then I goed to my class math at the Community College. I fall asleep in the class. Because I was very tired. Fortunately I didn't snore. My friend she woke me up.

_____

_____

_____

_____

_____

_____

_____

_____

_____

Answer with a complete sentence.

1. Where did the author take her baby? _____

_____

2. How long was the author's break? _____

_____

3. What are 3 irregular past tense verbs in this paragraph? _____

_____

4. What is the topic sentence of this paragraph? _____

_____

Writing Assignment 10: Preparing to write

Complete the chart. Describe what you did yesterday. Use the verbs below or other verbs. Use past tense verbs. Don't write complete sentences.

visit	sweep	cook	go (shopping)
work	vacuum	eat	drive
buy	do (the dishes)	drink	wait for
study	do (laundry)	watch	read
talk to	do (homework)	listen to (music)	send (email)
exercise	take care of	clean	text

Morning	Afternoon	Evening
_____	_____	_____
_____	_____	_____
_____	_____	_____
_____	_____	_____
_____	_____	_____

Writing Assignment 10: What I did yesterday

Write a paragraph about what you did yesterday.

1. In the top right corner of your paper write the heading.

2. Indent and write a topic sentence.

3. Skip lines.

4. Write between 7 and 10 sentences. Use the chart on the previous page to help you. Include interesting details. Do not include sentences like *I brushed my teeth* and *I took a shower.* Everyone does those things so they are not very interesting!

5. Write at least 1 compound sentence.

6. Use *because* in at least 1 sentence.

7. Write 1 negative sentence.

8. Use the editing checklist below to check your work. Circle *Yes* or *No* for each item in the checklist.

Writing Assignment 10: Editing Checklist

Editing Checklist		
Format		
1. I have a correct heading.	Yes	No
2. The first line is indented.	Yes	No
3. I skipped lines.	Yes	No
Content		
1. The paragraph has a topic sentence.	Yes	No
2. My paragraph has between 7 and 10 sentences.	Yes	No
3. My paragraph has at least 1 compound sentence.	Yes	Yes
4. My paragraph has at least 1 sentence that includes *because*.	Yes	Yes
5. My paragraph has at least 1 negative sentence.		
Capitalization and punctuation		
1. I used capital letters correctly.	Yes	No
2. I ended each sentence with a period.	Yes	No
Grammar		
1. All sentences have a subject and a verb.	Yes	No
2. I used past tense verbs correctly.	Yes	No
3. There are no run-on sentences.	Yes	No

Chapter 11

A Special Day

In this chapter you'll write about a special day.

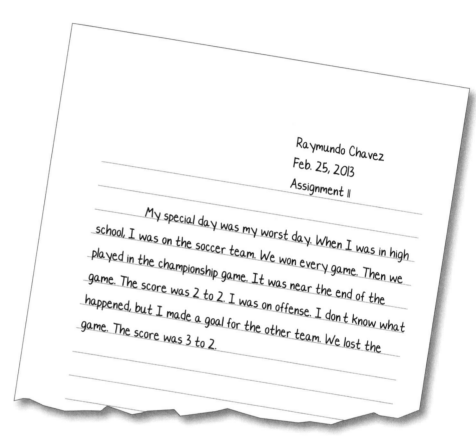

Raymundo Chavez
Feb. 25, 2013
Assignment 11

My special day was my worst day. When I was in high school, I was on the soccer team. We won every game. Then we played in the championship game. It was near the end of the game. The score was 2 to 2. I was on offense. I don't know what happened, but I made a goal for the other team. We lost the game. The score was 3 to 2.

Answer each question with a complete sentence.

1. What sport did Raymundo play in high school? _____

_____

2. Did Raymundo play offense or defense? _____

_____

3. What was the score at the end of the game? _____

_____

4. Did Raymundo's team win or lose? _____

_____

Vocabulary: Talking about special events

You often use these verbs to talk about events in your past. Study this list.

1. _____ be (born) _____	6. _____ get (pregnant) _____	11. _____ win (a game, a tournament) _____
2. _____ get (a job) _____	7. _____ have (a baby) _____	12. _____ celebrate (a birthday, an anniversary) _____
3. _____ get (a driver's license) _____	8. _____ meet (my wife, girlfriend, etc.) _____	13. _____ graduate (from elementary school, high school, etc.) _____
4. _____ get (married) _____	9. _____ move _____	14. _____ visit _____
5. _____ get (divorced) _____	10. _____ learn (to drive) _____	15. _____ immigrate _____

Talk about it/Think about it

- Read the verbs in the box above. Put a check next to each one you know.
- Learn the meanings of verbs you don't know. Ask your classmates or look up the words in a dictionary.
- Write the past tense of the verb on the line below the verb.

Talk about it

Choose 5 events from the box. Tell your partner the year they happened. Use past tense verbs. (For example, *I moved to the U.S. in 2009.*)

Write about it

Write 5 important events from your partner's life. Write the year they happened. (For example, *My partner met his girlfriend in 2010*.)

1. _____

2. _____

3. _____

4. _____

5. _____

Using *ago*

Use *ago* to show when something started. The structure is

> amount of time (**an hour**, **a day**, **a week**, etc.) + **ago**

Here are some examples:

> The class started <u>five minutes ago</u>.

> We had a test <u>a week ago</u>.

Talk about it

Ask your partner the following questions.

1. Where were you 15 minutes ago?

2. Where were you an hour ago?

3. Where were you three hours ago?

4. Where were you a year ago?

5. Where were you five years ago?

Using *last*

Use *last* before a time expression such as **night**, **week**, **month**, and **year**. For example

> I got married <u>last year</u>.

Practice 11.1: Complete each sentence with *ago* or *last*.

1. Lisa met her boyfriend _____ month.

2. I went to New York a year _____.

3. We visited my sister two weeks _____.

4. We went to Bolivia three years _____.

5. Fatima bought a computer _____ year.

6. Our rent was late _____ month.

7. The weather was very hot _____ year.

8. Yin left a few minutes _____.

9. We were at a party _____ night.

10. Your brother was here an hour _____.

Common mistakes with past tense verbs

When speaking about the past, don't use present tense verbs. Use past tense verbs.

Incorrect	Correct
Yesterday, I ~~work~~ all day.	Yesterday, I <u>worked</u> all day.

Don't add *ed* to irregular past tense verbs.

Incorrect	Correct
I ~~drinked~~ two cups of coffee yesterday.	I <u>drank</u> two cups of coffee yesterday.

Use *was* and *were* for the past tense of *to be.*

Incorrect	Correct
Laura ~~is~~ at work yesterday.	Laura <u>was</u> at work yesterday.

In negative past tense sentences, don't use a past tense verb. Use the base verb with *did not* or *didn't*.

Incorrect	Correct
We didn't ~~went~~ to Los Angeles.	We <u>didn't go</u> to Los Angeles.

Don't use *no* in negative past tense sentences.

Incorrect	Correct
I ~~no~~ buy soda.	I <u>didn't</u> buy soda.

Think about it

Work with a partner.

- If the sentence is correct, put an X in the *Correct* box.

- If the sentence is not correct, put an X in the *Incorrect* box. Then correct the sentence.

	Correct	Incorrect
was 1. The bus ~~is~~ late yesterday.		X
2. My brother got a new computer yesterday.		
3. My sister comed to my house yesterday.		
4. I didn't has a job last year.		
5. Last year, I lived in San Jose and work in San Francisco.		

	Correct	Incorrect
6. I no call you because I was sick.		
7. Angela brushed her hair, but she no brush her teeth.		
8. Yesterday I leave my keys in my car.		
9. Five years ago, I didn't speak English.		
10. Marcus study English two years ago.		
11. My daughter was sick yesterday, but I didn't stayed home.		
12. I no come to class yesterday.		
13. My boss called me last night.		
14. Angela's mother came to the U.S. seven years ago.		
15. The weather is cold and rainy last week.		
16. Two years ago I live in Guatemala.		
17. Last year Erica get very sick.		
18. Joanna start her new job a month ago.		
19. Your class started an hour ago.		
20. My partner no come to class today.		

Practice 11.2: In this paragraph there are 10 errors with affirmative and negative past tense verbs. Correct them.

I have a great time at the park yesterday. I goed there alone. I ran around the track a few times. Then I see my friend Chad. We talk for about 15 minutes. Then we meet our friends Mike and Juan. They want to play soccer with some other friends. We had a great game. I am the goalie. My team no win. It no was close. The score was five to zero. I was tired after the game, but I haved a very good time.

Time clauses with *before* and *after*

You use *before time clauses* and *after time clauses* to tell the order in which events happen. Here is the form.

Main clause	Time clause
I ate dinner	before I watched TV.
I ate dinner	after I watched TV.

Notice the following:

- The sentences have 2 clauses, a *main clause* and a *time clause*.
- The first word in the time clause is **before** or **after**. These words are *conjunctions* or joining words.
- The time clause has a subject and a verb. The main clause also has a subject and a verb.
- A time clause is *not* a complete sentence. It is not correct to say,

    ~~Before I ate dinner.~~

You also can start sentences with a time clause followed by the main clause. When you start a sentence with a time clause, put a comma after the time clause. The comma is *not* optional. Here is the form.

Time clause	Main clause
Before I ate dinner,	I watched TV.
After I ate dinner,	I watched TV.

Think about it

- Work with a partner.
- Read the paragraph below out loud.
- Underline each sentence that has a main clause and a time clause. There are a total of 5.
- Circle the conjunctions **before** and **after**.
- Answer the questions on the next page.

I felt very excited before I came to the U.S. I wanted to see the tall buildings. I wanted to go shopping. I wanted to attend an American school. Before I came to the U.S., I was also nervous. I didn't know very much English and I didn't have a job. I felt very lonely after I arrived. I missed my friends in my country. Everything was very expensive. The people spoke very quickly. After I was here for about a month, I met a girl from my hometown. After I had a good friend, everything was better.

1. Find 2 sentences in the paragraph that *start* with a *before* time clause or an *after* time clause. Write them below.

_____

_____

2. Find 2 sentences in the paragraph that *end* with a *before* time clause or an *after* time clause. Write them below.

_____

_____

3. How did the author feel before she came to the U.S.?_____

_____

4. How did the author feel immediately after she came to the U.S.?_____

_____

Time clauses with *when*

You use *when time clauses* to talk about 2 things that happened at the same time. Here is the form.

Main clause	Time clause
I felt nervous	when I started this class.

Time clause	Main clause
When I started this class,	I felt nervous.

Notice the following:

- Each sentence has 2 clauses, a *main clause* and a *time clause*.
- The first word in the time clause is **when**. **When** is a *conjunction* or a joining word.
- The time clause has a subject and a verb. The main clause has a subject and a verb.
- A time clause is *not* a complete sentence. It is not correct to say

  ~~When I started this class.~~

- When the time clause is at the beginning of a sentence, put a comma after it. The comma is *not* optional.

Think about it

- Work with a partner.
- Read the paragraph on the next page out loud.
- Underline each sentence that has a main clause and a *when* time clause. There are 4.
- Circle the conjunction **when**.
- Answer the questions.

When my cousin Lucy was a baby, she cried all the time. She cried when she went to the park. She cried when she went to her babysitter's house. She cried in her car seat. When she was nine months old, she started to crawl. Then she was happy. She didn't cry any more.

1. Write 2 sentences in the paragraph that *start* with a *when* time clause.

   _____

   _____

2. Write 2 sentences in the paragraph that *end* with a *when* time clause.

   _____

   _____

3. Did Lucy cry in her car seat? _____

   _____

4. What happened when Lucy was nine months old? _____

   _____

Practice 11.3: Do the following:

- Circle the conjunction ***when.***
- Put 2 lines under the verb in each clause. Put 1 line under the subject.
- Rewrite the sentence: If the time clause comes at the beginning of the sentence, put it at the end of the sentence. If the time clause comes at the end of the sentence, put it at the beginning of the sentence.

1. When I was five years old, I moved from Vietnam. I moved from Viet Nam when I was five years old.

2. I was 23 when I got my driver's license. _____

   _____

3. My parents were very excited when I graduated from high school. _____

   _____

4. When my sister visited, we stayed up late every night. _____

   _____

5. Jose got a reward when he found the missing wallet. _____

   _____

Complete and incomplete sentences

A time clause that starts with *before*, *after*, or *when* has a subject and a verb. But a time clause is *not* a complete sentence.

Think about it

Work with a partner. Check whether each of the following is a complete sentence or an incomplete sentence.

	Complete	Incomplete
1. Before I went to work.		X
2. I got married after I came to the U.S.		
3. After I came to the U.S.		
4. Rudolph flew to Alaska on Tuesday.		
5. When I lived in San Francisco.		
6. Before class started, I had a cup of coffee.		
7. Before class started.		
8. I had a cup of coffee.		
9. We worked eight hours.		
10. After we worked eight hours.		

Think about it

Do the following:

- If the sentence is correct, check the *Correct* box.

- If the sentence is not correct, check the *Incorrect* box. Correct the sentence.

	Correct	Incorrect
1. Before I worked at Target, I worked at Ross.	X	
2. When we went to the beach. We had a picnic.		
3. Bob went to the grocery store after he went to the bank.		
4. Jose's grades improved. After he moved to a new school.		
5. Before Linda got married, she lived by herself.		
6. I moved to Colorado. After I lived in the Nevada for four years.		
7. When I was a child I liked to play outside.		

Talk about it

Talk to your partner. Start each sentence with the following clauses.

1. Before I came to class, I _____

2. Before I went to bed last night, I_____

3. After I got home last night, I _____

4. After I ate dinner last night, I _____

5. When I started this class, _____

Write about it

Complete the following sentences.

1. Before I _____

_____

2. After I _____

_____

3. Before my brother _____

_____

4. After my sister _____

_____

5. When I _____

_____

Adding a title to a paragraph

The *title* of a paragraph tells what the paragraph is about. The title is usually not a sentence. The following is a good title for a paragraph about a dog.

My Wonderful Dog

Titles usually do not include verbs. This isn't a good title:

My Dog Is Wonderful

Here are rules for using capital letters in a title:

- The first word of the title is always capitalized.

- All other words in the title are capitalized except for little words such as *a*, *an*, *in*, *at*, *on*, and *the*.

Think about it

- Read each paragraph.
- Underline the topic sentence.
- Circle the best title for the paragraph.

Paragraph 1

My first day of school in the U.S. was very difficult. When I walked into the classroom, it was empty. I sat alone at a table. When more students entered, they didn't sit with me. I felt extremely lonely. When the teacher spoke English, I didn't understand anything. I felt stupid. After the class ended, I went home and cried. Fortunately, the next day of class was better.

What is the best title for this paragraph?

A. My First Day of School in the U.S.

B. My First Day of School Was Difficult

C. Schools in the U.S.

D. My Classroom

Paragraph 2

My wedding was very special. It was in a small church in my hometown. When I woke up on my wedding day, it was sunny. My mother and sister helped me put on my wedding dress. It was a long, white dress with a lace collar and a veil. My cousin did my hair. After I got dressed, I was a little afriad. After the wedding ceremony, I felt wonderful. We had a big party, and I danced all night. I went to sleep at 4 a.m.

What is the best title for this paragraph?

A. My Wedding Dress

B. My Wedding Day

C. I Had a Great Wedding

D. Weddings in My Country

Paragraph 3

My mother died five years ago. I was 17 years old. When she died, we lived in Mexico. My mother was very sick before she died. I stayed with her. I cooked her food and gave her baths. Before she died, she told me stories about her life. I wrote the stories in a book. Now I read the stories to my daughter.

What is the best title for this paragraph?

A. My Mother

B. I Stayed With my Mother Before She Died

C. Death in my Family

D. My Mother's Last Days

Editing challenge

Now you're ready to practice what you've learned.

- Read the paragraph.
- Correct the errors. Each error is underlined.
- Rewrite the paragraph.
- Answer the questions on the next page.

The Birth of my <u>daughter</u>

My daughter ＿＿ born on <u>august 2</u> 1987. She <u>arrive</u> three weeks late. At 11:00 p.m. on <u>august</u> 1 I felt <u>pains bad</u>. When I told my <u>husband</u> he <u>no</u> believed me. The pains <u>continue</u>. When I <u>scream</u> with pain, my husband <u>believe</u> me. We <u>drive</u> to the hospital. I screamed in the car, and <u>My</u> <u>husband he</u> drove very fast. After I <u>arrive</u> at the hospital, I <u>go</u> to the <u>section</u> <u>maternity</u>. The <u>pains they</u> got <u>more worse</u>. The doctor and the nurse <u>comed</u> quickly<u>,</u> <u>one</u> hour later my baby was born. She was a miracle.

_____

_____

_____

_____

_____

_____

_____

_____

_____

_____

Answer with a complete sentence.

1. What is the title of this paragraph? _____

_____

2. What is the topic sentence of this paragraph? _____

_____

3. Did the baby arrive early or late? _____

_____

4. Who drove the author to the hospital? _____

_____

5. Write a sentence in the paragraph that has a **when** clause. _____

_____

Writing Assignment 11: Preparing to write

Write about a special day or event in your life. Use the list of verbs on the first page of this chapter to help you.

1. What day or event will you write about? _____

2. Write 8 verbs that tell what happened that day. Use past tense verbs. Do not write complete sentences.

a. _____

b. _____

c. _____

d. _____

e. _____

f _____

g. _____

h. _____

Writing Assignment 11: *A Special Day*

Write a paragraph about a special day.

1. In the top right corner of your paper write the heading.

2. Write a title.

3. Indent and write a topic sentence.

4. Skip lines.

5. Write at least 10 sentences.

6. Write at least 2 sentences that have a time clause that starts with **when**, **before**, or **after**.

7. Use the editing checklist to check your work. Circle **Yes** or **No** for each item in the checklist.

Writing Assignment 11: Editing Checklist

Editing Checklist		
Format		
1. I have a correct heading.	Yes	No
2. The first line is indented.	Yes	No
3. I skipped lines.	Yes	No
Content		
1. The paragraph has a title.	Yes	No
2. The paragraph has a topic sentence.	Yes	No
3. My paragraph has at least 10 sentences.	Yes	No
4. My paragraph has at least 2 sentences that have a time clause that starts with **when**, **before**, or **after**.	Yes	No
Capitalization and punctuation		
1. I used capital letters correctly.	Yes	No
2. I ended each sentence with a period.	Yes	No
Grammar		
1. All sentences have a subject and a verb.	Yes	No
2. I used past tense verbs correctly.	Yes	No
3. There are no run-on sentences.	Yes	No

Chapter 12

The Vacation of My Dreams

In this chapter you'll write about the vacation of your dreams.

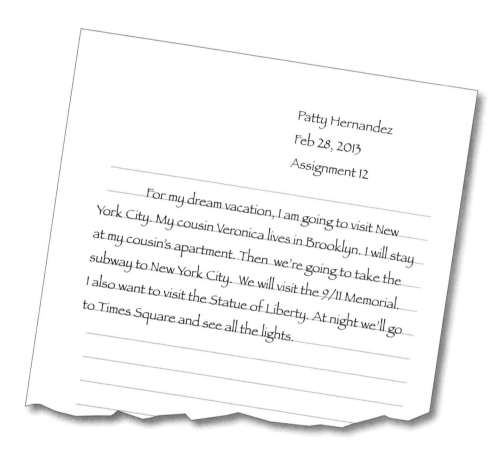

Patty Hernandez
Feb 28, 2013
Assignment 12

For my dream vacation, I am going to visit New York City. My cousin Veronica lives in Brooklyn. I will stay at my cousin's apartment. Then we're going to take the subway to New York City. We will visit the 9/11 Memorial. I also want to visit the Statue of Liberty. At night we'll go to Times Square and see all the lights.

Answer each question with a complete sentence.

1. Where will Patty go for her dream vacation? _____

_____

2. Where does Patty's cousin live? _____

_____

3. How will Patty and Veronica get to New York City from Veronica's apartment? _____

_____

4. Where will Patty and Veronica go at night? _____

_____

The future tense: *to be* + *going* + infinitive

Earlier you learned that an infinitive has this form.

to + base verb

You use *to be* + *going* + infinitivie to talk about plans and predictions for the future. For example,

I <u>am going to watch</u> TV after dinner.

Tomorrow we <u>are going to have</u> a busy day.

Here is the form.

Subject	Verb to be	going	infinitive	rest of sentence
I	am			
He /She/ It	is	going	to eat	pizza tomorrow.
You /We/ They	are			

You also can use contractions when you talk about the future. Here is the form.

Contraction	going	infinitive	rest of sentence
I'm			
He's/She's/It's	going	to eat	pizza tomorrow.
You're/We're/They're			

Practice 12.1: Complete the sentences with the correct form of *to be* + *going to* followed by the verb in parentheses ().

1. (sleep) I _____ am going to sleep _____ late tomorrow.

2. (play) Juana _____ basketball tomorrow.

3. (visit) Ning _____ his sister tomorrow.

4. (take) We _____ a test tomorrow.

5. (interview) My boss _____ my friend Lucy tomorrow.

6. (call) My brother and I _____ our parents tomorrow.

7. (go shopping) My daughter and I _____ tomorrow.

8. (graduate) I _____ from high school next year.

9. (improve) The U.S. economy _____ next year.

10. (be) Max and Arturo _____ in Los Angeles tomorrow.

11. (listen to) After work, we _____ music.

12. (be, visit) My daughter _____ happy tomorrow

because we _____ her favorite cousins.

Write about it

Work with a partner. Complete the sentences. Use **to be + going** and one of the phrases in the box.

to talk to my teacher	to study	to call the dentist
to eat salad for dinner	to go shopping	to take my umbrella
to go to the post office	to call the doctor	to take a nap
to do the laundry	to wash my car	to make dinner

1. I don't understand the homework. I <u>am going to talk to my teacher.</u>

2. My sister has a high fever. She _____

3. Angela needs new shoes. She _____

4. Han has a toothache. He _____

5. We need to mail a package. We _____

6. The students have a test tomorrow. They _____

7. Vinnie and Ana are on a diet. They _____

8. My family is hungry. I _____

9. Fernando is tired. He _____

10. It is going to rain. I _____

11. Mario doesn't have any clean clothes. He _____

12. My car is filthy. I _____

Using *to be* + *going* + infinitive correctly

Use only 1 verb after **to be** + **going** + **infinitive**. This sentence is correct.

> I am going <u>to clean</u> my house tonight.

Do not say

> I am going ~~to go clean~~ my house tonight.

Think about it

Correct this paragraph. Cross out the word **go** when it is not necessary. The first sentence is corrected for you.

Tomorrow I am going to ~~go~~ visit my sister. She is sick. I am going to go take care of her. We are going to go watch TV together. After that, I am going to go clean her house. I am going to go cook dinner for her family. Then I am going to go wash the dishes.

Talk about it

Work with a partner. Tell your partner 5 things you are going to do tomorrow. Use *to be* + *going to* in every sentence.

Common mistakes with *to be* + *going* + *infinitive*

You must include *to be* before *going*.

Incorrect	Correct
Tomorrow, I ~~going to visit~~ my mother.	Tomorrow I **am** <u>going to visit</u> my mother.
	Tomorrow I**'m** <u>going to</u> visit my mother.

You must include *to* before the base verb.

Incorrect	Correct
We are ~~going play~~ soccer tomorrow.	We <u>are going</u> **to** <u>play</u> soccer tomorrow.

Put the *base form* of the verb after *to*.

Incorrect	Correct
Juan is going to ~~watching~~ TV now.	Juan is going to <u>watch</u> TV now.

Think about it

Work with a partner.

- If the sentence is correct, put an X in the *Correct* box.
- If the sentence is not correct, put an X in the *Incorrect* box. Then correct the sentence. Some sentences have more than one error.

	Correct	Incorrect
<u>are</u> 1. We going to make tamales tomorrow.		X
2. Angela is going wash her car tomorrow.		
3. The students are going to go have a party tomorrow.		

	Correct	Incorrect
4. I am going to take the bus tomorrow morning.		
5. Fred going drive his car.		
6. We going play soccer tomorrow.		
7. They are going exercise after class.		
8. My brother and I are going play cards tomorrow.		
9. My boss is going to go to be late tomorrow.		
10. Lourdes going to studying engineering in her country.		
11. They are going to go watch TV after dinner.		
12. Ning and Len are going drive to work together.		

Negative sentences with *to be* + *going* + *infinitive*

To make a negative sentence with *to be* + *going* + infinitive, add *not* after the verb *to be*. Study the form.

Subject	Verb **to be**	**not**	**going**	infinitive	Rest of sentence
I	am				
He /She/ It	is	not	going	to eat	pizza tomorrow.
You /We/ They	are				

You also can use contractions in negative future tense sentences.

Subject + Contraction	**not**	**going**	infinitive	Rest of sentence
I'm				
He's/She's/It's	not	going	to eat	pizza tomorrow.
You're/We're/They're				

You also can use this form.

Subject + Contraction	**going**	infinitive	Rest of sentence
I'm not			
She isn't /He isn't/It isn't	going	to eat	pizza tomorrow.
You aren't/We aren't/They aren't			

Practice 12.2: Make each sentence negative. Use contractions where you can. Some sentences are not future tense.

1. I am going to study English. _____

_____

2. We're going to play cards this afternoon. _____

_____

3. The children are ready for class. _____

_____

4. Angela is going to drive to work today. _____

_____

5. I was sick yesterday. _____

_____

6. She's going to leave at 5:00. _____

_____

7. We visited our parents last week. _____

_____

8. My parents are going to take care of my daughter tomorrow. _____

_____

9. Lucy is going to plant her garden tomorrow. _____

_____

Talk about it

Work with a partner. Tell your partner 3 things you are going to do this weekend and 3 things you are *not* going to do this weekend. For example, *I am going to wash my car. I'm not going to clean my house.*

go shopping	have a party	run
clean my house	go to a party	go to the gym
wash my car	play soccer	call my family
exercise	do laundry	do homework
visit friends	visit my family	play with my children
go dancing	buy food	send email

Talking about the future

Here are some time expressions you use to talk about the future.

this...	tomorrow...	next...	in...
this morning	tomorrow morning	the next day	in a minute, in a few minutes
this afternoon	tomorrow afternoon	next week	in an hour, in a few hours
this evening	tomorrow evening	next month	in a few days
	the day after tomorrow	next year	in a week, in a few weeks, in a month, in a few months, etc.

You use expressions like *this morning* and *this afternoon* to talk about things that are going to happen that day.

> <u>This morning</u> I am going to take a test.

Put future time expressions at the beginning of the sentence or at the end of the sentence. If the future time expression is at the beginning of a sentence, you can put a comma after it. The comma is optional.

> I am going to play basketball <u>tomorrow</u>.

> <u>Tomorrow</u>, I am going to play basketball.

> <u>Tomorrow</u> I am going to play basketball.

Do not put the time expression in the middle of the sentence.

> I ~~tomorrow~~ am going to play basketball.

> I am going ~~tomorrow~~ to play basketball.

Practice 12.3: Make the words in parentheses into a sentence. Place the time expression at the beginning or the end of the sentence.

1. (am going to, next week, I, new shoes, buy) _____

_____

1. (visit, next year, are going to, we, Mexico) _____

_____

2. (is going to, this afternoon, play basketball, Mario) _____

_____

3. (Ana, is going to, the day after tomorrow, go shopping) _____

_____

4. (be, am going to, in five years, I, rich) _____

_____

6. (move, next week, are going to, they) _____

_____

7. (is going to, tonight, her birthday, celebrate, Min) _____

_____

8. (change jobs, Max, is going to, in a few months) _____

_____

9. (is going to, call, later today, Sid) _____

_____

Talk about it

Tell you partner what you are going to do in the future using the future time expressions in the box below. (For example, *Next year, I am going to visit the Dominican Republic*.)

tonight	tomorrow morning	in a few days
in a few hours	tomorrow afternoon	next year

Talk about it

Repeat the previous exercise. Talk about a family member or friend. (For example, *In a few hours, my wife is going to pick up my son at school.*)

The future tense: *will*

In general, you use both *will* and *to be + going* to talk about the future. For example you can say

I <u>am going to</u> work tomorrow.

I <u>will</u> work tomorrow.

You will learn about a few differences between *will* and *to be + going to* in a more advanced English class. For now, use both to talk about the future. Study the form.

Subject	will	Base verb	Rest of the sentence
I /You/He/She/It/We/They	will	live	to be 100 years old.

You also can use contractions.

Subject	Base verb	Rest of the sentence
I'll/You'll/ He'll/ She'll/ We'll/They'll	live	to be 100 years old.

There is no contraction ~~It'll~~.

Write about it

Write 5 things you will do to help around the house this weekend. Use **will** in each sentence.

1. _____

2. _____

3. _____

4. _____

5. _____

Negative sentences with *will*

Negative sentences with **will** have this form.

Subject	will	not	Base verb	Rest of the sentence
I /You/He/She/It/We/They	will	not	live	to be 100 years old.

Instead of **will not**, you can use **won't**.

Subject	won't	Base verb	Rest of the sentence
I /You/He/She/It/We/They	won't	live	to be 100 years old.

Think about it

Work with a partner. Make predictions for the year 2030. Use **will** or **won't**.

1. Most people _____ live to be 100 years old.

2. We _____ have a cure for cancer.

3. Everyone _____ have a computer.

4. Most people _____ drive electric cars.

5. People _____ live on the moon.

6. Children _____ go to school six days a week.

7. Immigrants in the United States _____ have a better life.

8. The United States _____ have a woman president.

9. People _____ live on Mars.

10. All food _____ be organic.

Common mistakes with *will*

Put the *base form* of the verb after **will**.

Incorrect	Correct
The bus ~~will coming soon~~.	The bus <u>will come</u> soon.
The bus ~~will comes~~ soon.	

In negative sentences, place **not** after **will** or use **won't**.

Incorrect	Correct
The bus ~~no will come~~ soon.	The bus <u>will not come</u> soon.
The bus ~~will no come~~ soon.	The bus <u>won't come</u> soon.

Think about it

Work with a partner.

- If the sentence is correct, put an X in the *Correct* box.
- If the sentence is not correct, put an X in the *Incorrect* box. Then correct the sentence.

	Correct	Incorrect
1. We will win the soccer game.	X	
2. I will helps you.		
3. The United States will no elect a woman president.		
4. I will washing the floor.		
5. My daughter will graduating from college.		
6. I will pass this class.		
7. My husband will remember my birthday.		
8. Juan no will come to school tomorrow.		
9. Park will no get a new job.		
10. Blanca and Jerome no will get married.		

Using *to be* in the past, present, and future

The verb *to be* can be used in 2 ways.

- As the main verb in a sentence or clause

- As the auxiliary verb in a sentence or clause

When *to be* is used in the simple present and the simple past, it is the *main* verb in the sentence or clause. It is the *only* verb in the sentence or clause. Study these examples.

Verb tense	Examples: *To be* as a main verb
Simple past	I **was** at home last night. Nadira **was** at work yesterday, but she **was** sick.
Simple present	I **am** ready. You **are** late again.

When *to be* is used in the present continuous and future tenses, it is an *auxiliary verb*. That is, it is used with another verb. Study these examples.

Verb tense	Examples: *To be* as an auxiliary verb
Present continuous	I **am** working now. Pablo and Jerome **are** playing volleyball with their friends.
Future (*will*)	I **will** arrive at 3:30. The students **will** take the final exam on Monday.
Future (*to be + going to*)	We **are** going to take a break at 10:00. My mother **is** going to bake a cake for my birthday.

Think about it

Work with a partner. Read these sentences with *to be.* Put 2 lines under the verb and 1 line under the subject. Then write *past*, *present*, or *future*.

1. I was tired last night. ____past____

2. Ana is at the park. _____

3. I am reading a book now. _____

4. We will visit our cousin tomorrow. _____

5. I am at home. _____

6. They were sick last week. _____

7. I was in Chicago when you were in Detroit. _____

8. The children will play outside at 3:00. _____

9. My parents were born in Russia, but I was born in the US. _____

10. Bernard is going to go home at 8:00. _____

Future time clauses with *before, after,* and *when*

You use *before time clauses, after time clauses,* and *when time clauses* to tell the order in which events happen in the future. Here is the form.

Main clause (future tense)	Time clause (present tense)
I am going to study	**before** I visit my sister.
I will study	**before** I visit my sister.
I am going to study	**after** I visit my sister.
I will study	**after** I visit my sister.
I am going to study	**when** I visit my sister.
I will study	**when** I visit my sister.

Notice the following:

- Each sentence has 2 clauses, a *main clause* and a *time clause*.
- You use the future tense in the main clause.
- You use the present tense in the time clause.

You also can start sentences with a time clause. When you start a sentence with a time clause, the time clause has a comma after it. Here is the form.

Time clause (present tense)	Main clause (future tense)
Before I visit my sister,	I am going to study.
Before I visit my sister,	I will study.
After I visit my sister,	I am going to study.
After I visit my sister,	I will study.
When I visit my sister,	I am going to study.
When I visit my sister,	I will study.

Think about it

- Work with a partner.
- Read the paragraph on the next page out loud.
- Put 2 lines under each verb. Write *P* if the verb is in the present tense and *F* if the verb is in future tense.
- Put 1 line under the subject.
- Circle the conjunctions *before, after,* or *when*.
- Answer the questions.

                                      F

Tomorrow I am going to go to San Francisco with my girlfriend. We are going to take the train. After I get on the train, I am going to relax and talk to my girlfriend. After we arrive at the station, we are going to take a bus to Golden Gate Park. When we get to the park, we are going to meet my cousins. Then, we'll have a picnic. We will go out to eat dinner at an Italian restaurant before we take the train home.

Answer with a complete sentence.

1. Where is the author going to go? _____

_____

2. Where is the author going to eat dinner? _____

_____

3. Write a sentence in this paragraph that has a time clause. _____

_____

Write about it

Complete each sentence. Use **to be + going to** in the main clause. Tell the truth.

1. After I watch TV, I _____ am going to take a shower. _____

2. When I get home this evening, I _____

3. After I get up tomorrow morning, I _____

4. Before I go to bed tonight, I _____

5. When I complete this class, I _____

Practice 12.4

- Read the paragraph.
- Put 2 lines under each verb. Put 1 line under each subject.
- Write *P* if the verb is in the present tense.
- Write *F* if the verb is in the future tense.
- Circle the conjunctions. There are 4.

                                    F

For my dream vacation, I am going to visit Seoul, Korea because I miss it very much. First I will visit my friends. They are students at the university. We will go to Gangnam Street. It's a very busy street and it has a lot of night life. After we eat dinner, we'll go dancing. The next day I will visit my cousins. They live on the 28th floor of a tall apartment building. We will eat Korean barbecue in their neighborhood. Then we will go to Myeongdong. I will look at the beautiful clothes, but I won't buy anything. All of the stores are very expensive.

Editing challenge

Now you're ready to practice what you've learned.

- Correct the errors in this paragraph. Each error is underlined.
- Rewrite the paragraph.
- Answer the questions on the next page.

My Dream Vacation

For my dream vacation, I <u>return</u> to my hometown in <u>Puebla</u> Mexico. When I <u>will arrive</u> at my house, I will see my <u>mother my</u> father, my brother, _____ my grandmother. My mother will _____ very happy. She <u>going</u> to give me a <u>hug big</u>. My <u>Father</u> is not going to talk a lot <u>because is</u> a <u>person quiet</u>. My <u>brother he</u> will show me the new TV. My <u>grandmother very</u> old, but she <u>have</u> a lot of energy. She is <u>going cook</u> mole. After we eat dinner_ we <u>watch</u> TV. I will <u>describing</u> my life in the US.

My Dream Vacation

_____

_____

_____

_____

_____

_____

_____

_____

_____

Answer with a complete sentence.

1. What is the title of this paragraph? _____

   _____

2. What is the topic sentence of this paragraph? _____

   _____

3. Where will the author go on her dream vacation? _____

   _____

4. Who will the author see? _____

   _____

5. What is her brother going to do? _____

   _____

6. What will her grandmother cook? _____

   _____

7. Write a sentence from the paragraph that has a *when* clause. _____

   _____

Writing Assignment 12: Preparing to write

Use the graphic organizer on the next page to plan your paragraph.

- Write your destination in the middle circle.
- Write one thing you will do on your dream vacation in each section of the circle. Start with section 1. You don't need to write a complete sentence!

Graphic Organizer: The Vacation of my Dreams

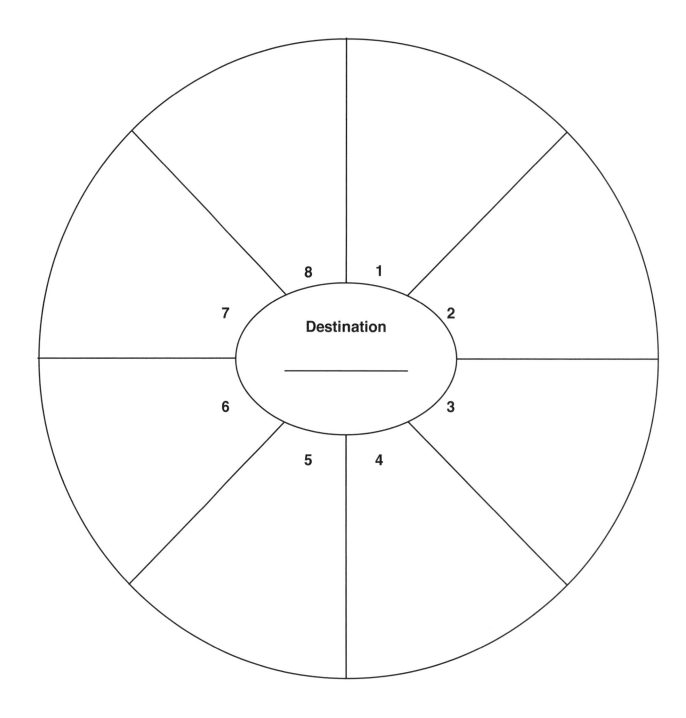

Writing Assignment 12: My Dream Vacation

Write a paragraph about your dream vacation.

1. In the top right corner of your paper write the heading.

2. Write a title.

3. Indent and write a topic sentence.

4. Skip lines.

5. Write at least 8 sentences.

6. Write at least 2 sentences that have a time clause that starts with *when*, *before*, or *after*.

7. Use at least 2 time order words: *first*, *next*, *then*, *after that*, *later*, or *finally*.

8. Use the editing checklist to check your work. Circle *Yes* or *No* for each item in the checklist.

Writing Assignment 12: Editing checklist

Editing Checklist		
Format		
1. I have a correct heading.	Yes	No
2. The first line is indented.	Yes	No
3. I skipped lines.	Yes	No
Content		
1. The paragraph has a title.	Yes	No
2. The paragraph has a topic sentence.	Yes	No
3. My paragraph has at least 10 sentences.	Yes	No
4. My paragraph has at least 2 sentences that have a time clause that starts with *when*, *before*, or *after*.	Yes	No
5. My paragraph has at least 2 time order words: *first*, *next*, *then*, *after that*, *later*, or *finally*.	Yes	No
Capitalization and punctuation		
1. I used capital letters correctly.	Yes	No
2. I ended each sentence with a period.	Yes	No
Grammar		
1. All sentences have a subject and a verb.	Yes	No
2. I used future tense verbs.	Yes	No
3. There are no run-on sentences.	Yes	No

Spelling Rules: Plural Nouns and Simple Present Tense Verbs

Rule	Singular noun	Plural noun
For most nouns and verbs, add **s**.	*ball*	*balls*
	girl	*girls*
	speak	*speaks*
For nouns and verbs that end in **ch**, **s**, **sh**, **x**, or **z**, add **es**.	*class*	*classes*
	church	*churches*
	watch	*watches*
For nouns and verbs that end in a consonant + **y**, change the **y** to **i** and add **es**.	*baby*	*babies*
	cherry	*cherries*
	carry	*carries*

Spelling Rules: Present Participles

Rule	Base form	Present participle
For most verbs, add **ing**.	*work*	*working*
	talk	*talking*
	play	*playing*
For verbs that end in a consonant + **e**, delete the **e** and add **ing**.	*write*	*writing*
	dance	*dancing*
	take	*taking*
For verbs that end in a consonant + a vowel + a consonant, double the consonant.	*sit*	*sitting*
	run	*running*
	hit	*hitting*
Do not double the consonant if the verb ends in **w**, **x**, or **y**.	*play*	*playing*

Spelling Rules: Comparative Adjectives

Rule	Adjective	Comparative adjective
For most one syllable adjectives, add **er**.	*small*	*smaller*
	nice	*nicer*
	hard	*harder*
For adjectives that end in a consonant + a vowel + a consonant, double the consonant.	*big*	*bigger*
	hot	*hotter*
	flat	*flatter*
For one and two syllable adjectives that end in **y**, change **y** to **i** and add **er**.	*happy*	*happier*
	silly	*sillier*
	friendly	*friendlier*
For adjectives that are two or more syllables, use **more** before the adjective.	*interesting*	*more interesting*
	beautiful	*more beautiful*
	selfish	*more selfish*

Appendix B: Irregular Past Tense Verbs

Base form	Simple past	Base form	Simple past
be	was, were	leave	left
begin	began	lend	lent
become	became	lose	lost
break	broke	make	made
bring	brought	meet	met
build	built	pay	paid
buy	bought	put	put
choose	chose	read (like *need*)	read (like *red*)
come	came	ride	rode
drink	drank	run	ran
drive	drove	say	said
eat	ate	see	saw
fall	fell	sell	sold
feel	felt	send	sent
fight	fought	sing	sang
find	found	sit	sat
fly	flew	sleep	slept
forget	forgot	speak	spoke
get	got	spend	spent
give	gave	swim	swam
go	went	take	took
grow	grew	teach	taught
have	had	tell	told
hear	heard	think	thought
hit	hit	understand	understood
hold	held	wake up	woke up
hurt	hurt	wear	wore
keep	kept	win	won
know	knew	write	wrote

adjective: A word that modifies or describes a noun or pronoun. Examples of adjectives are *handsome*, *tired*, and *blue*.

adverb: A word that describes an adjective, verb or other adverb. Examples of adverbs are *always* and *very*.

adverb of frequency: An adverb that tells how often something occurs. *Always* and *sometimes* are adverbs of frequency.

auxiliary verb: A verb that is used with a main verb. Examples of auxiliary verbs are *do*, *does*, *am, is,* and *are*.

base verb: A verb that can be used alone or with an auxiliary verb. In this sentence, *I do not like pizza*, *like* is the base verb. Also called *main verb*.

clause: A group of related words with a subject and a verb.

comparative adjective: An adjective that compares nouns or pronouns. Examples are *bigger, better,* and *more important.*

compound sentence: A sentence with two or more clauses. Each clause has a subject and a verb and is a complete sentence. Clauses are joined by a conjunction such as *and* or *but*.

conjunction: A word that connects other words. Examples of conjunctions are *and*, *but*, and *because*.

contraction: A word that is formed by combining two other words. *I'm* and *isn't* are contractions.

demonstrative adjective: An adjective that tells whether something is near or far. The demonstrative adjectives are *this*, *that*, *these*, and *those*.

gender: A classification system that defines nouns, pronouns and adjectives as masculine, feminine or neuter. In English, gender only applies to a few nouns such as *mother* and *father*.

header: Information about the author that usually is in the upper right corner of an essay.

infinitive: A base verb preceded by *to*. Examples of infinitives are *to work* and *to study*.

irregular verb: A verb that does not follow the usual spelling rules. For example, irregular past tense verbs do not end in *ed*.

main verb: A verb that can be used alone or with an auxiliary verb. In this sentence, *I do not like pizza*, *like* is the main verb. Also called *base verb*.

non-action verb: A verb that does not show action. Examples of non-action verbs are *need*, *want*, and *like.* Also called *stative verbs.*

noun: A person, place, animal or thing. Examples of nouns are *teacher*, *book*, and *park*.

paragraph: A group of sentences about the same topic.

phrase: A group of related words that does not have a subject and a verb. Examples are *in the morning* and *on the floor*.

plural noun: A noun that refers to more than one person, place, animal, or thing. **Books** is a plural noun.

possessive adjective: An adjective that shows that something belongs to or is related to a noun. The possessive adjectives are **my**, **your**, **his**, **her**, **its**, **our**, and **their**.

possessive noun: A word that is used to show that something belongs to someone or something else. For example, in the sentence **Juana's sofa is new, Juana's** is the possessive noun because it shows that the sofa belongs to Juana.

preposition: A word that describes time, place, direction, or location. **In**, **over**, **to**, **at**, **on**, and **next to** are prepositions.

present continuous: A verb tense that is used to talk about activities that are happening right now. Also called *present progressive*. A present continuous verb includes **to be** and a participle. For example, **I am working now.** Also called *present progressive*.

present participle: A word that ends in **ing**. Examples of participles are **walking** and **thinking**. A present continuous verb must include a present participle.

present progressive: A verb tense that is used to talk about activities that are happening right now. A present progressive verb includes **to be** and a participle. For example, **I am working now.** Also called *present continuous*.

pronoun: A word that takes the place of a noun. (See *subject pronoun*.)

regular verb: A verb that follows the usual spelling rules.

simple present: A verb tense that is used to talk about habitual activities that occur in the present. For example, **I work five days a week.**

singular noun: A noun that refers to one person, place, animal or thing. **Book** is a singular noun.

stative verb: A verb that does not show action. Examples of stative verbs are **need, want,** and **like**. Also called **non-action verbs.**

subject: The word or words in the sentence that tell who or what the sentence is about. In this sentence, **Ana is married**, the subject is **Ana**.

subject pronoun: A pronoun that is the subject of a sentence. The subject pronouns are **I, you**, **he, she, it, we** and **they**.

topic sentence: The first sentence in a paragraph. The topic sentence tells what the paragraph is about.

verb: A word that shows action or state of being. Examples are **talk**, **sing**, **play**, and **is**.

verb tense: The form of the verb that tells whether the verb occurs in the past, present or future.